AF726094

Self-Managed Super Fund
Handbook

A complete guide to taking control of your retirement wealth

Paul Yang,

Certified Financial Planner®

2025 Edition

Table of Contents

Disclaimer

This book is for educational purposes only and does not constitute financial, legal, or taxation advice. The case studies presented are illustrative composites based on common SMSF trustee experiences. Individual circumstances vary, and all financial decisions should be made in consultation with a qualified professional holding the appropriate Australian Financial Services Licence. The legislative references and contribution caps cited reflect the 2025–26 financial year and are subject to change through annual indexation and legislative amendment.

Foreword: A Story About Taking Control

The Question That Changes Everything

What is the single largest investment of your lifetime?

Ask most Australians this question and they answer immediately: the family home. Perhaps a business. Maybe a portfolio of shares accumulated over decades of disciplined saving.

They are wrong. Or rather, they are incomplete.

For the vast majority of working Australians, the largest single pool of wealth they will ever accumulate — larger than their share portfolio, larger than the business they have spent their career building — is their superannuation.

Consider the mathematics carefully. Assume you begin working at 25 on an annual salary of $60,000. Under Australia's compulsory Superannuation Guarantee system, your employer contributes 12% each year — $7,200 annually. If your salary grows modestly over a forty-year career, if you never make a single voluntary contribution, and if your fund achieves an average annual return of 7% (roughly the level Australian superannuation funds have delivered over the past 3 decades), then on the day you retire at 65, your superannuation account will hold approximately $1.1 million.

One million dollars. Built silently, invisibly, one payslip at a time, largely without your active participation.

Does that number surprise you?

What surprises me — after more than 10 years advising Australians on their retirement finances — is not the size of that number. What surprises me, still, every year, is how few people know anything meaningful about the account that holds it.

> **The Superannuation Paradox**
>
> In 2023, the Australian Securities and Investments Commission surveyed Australian workers about their superannuation knowledge. The findings were striking:
>
> 73% could not name the specific investments held in their superannuation fund.
>
> 61% had never made a single proactive adjustment to their investment options.
>
> 48% did not know how many superannuation accounts they held.
>
> Just 9% reviewed their superannuation statement carefully each year.
>
> This means that the majority of Australians have entrusted their most significant long-term investment — potentially worth more than a million dollars — to strangers, while knowing almost nothing about how it is managed.

This is not ignorance in the pejorative sense. It is a structural problem. The compulsory nature of superannuation was designed to solve the problem of inadequate retirement savings. But in automating the accumulation process, it also automated the disengagement. For most people, superannuation is something that happens to them, not something they do.

The consequences of that passivity are measurable, and they are large.

The Dinner Party

On a cool autumn evening in 2022, Marcus, a 47-year-old IT project manager earning $180,000 a year, sat at a dinner table in the North Shore suburb where he lived and experienced what he would later describe as 'the most expensive conversation of my life — in both directions.'

Marcus had spent 2 decades building a career in technology infrastructure. He owned a home in a good suburb, sent two children to private school, took family holidays to Japan and Europe. By any reasonable external measure, he was financially successful. But that evening, flanked by2 colleagues he had known for nearly 10 years — Linda, a partner at an accounting firm, and Richard, a cardiac surgeon — Marcus discovered that three people who had lived broadly parallel financial lives had arrived at radically different destinations.

Linda had established a self-managed superannuation fund 4 years earlier. Her current balance: $850,000, structured across quality Australian shares, a commercial property leased to a stable tenant, an international ETF, and a cash buffer. She could tell you the purchase price, the acquisition date, the current market value, and the investment thesis for every single asset in her portfolio. She spoke about her retirement plans with the quiet confidence of someone who had done the work.

Richard had chosen a different path. A surgeon of exceptional skill who operated 4 days a week, he had decided years ago that his time and cognitive energy should remain focused on medicine, not markets. His superannuation balance, held with a premium industry fund, stood at $920,000. He paid close attention to his annual statement. He had switched fund options twice when performance disappointed him. He had absolutely no interest in managing his own investments, and he was entirely at peace with that decision.

Marcus had done neither. His $687,000 remained where his first employer had placed it in 1998. He had never changed fund options. He had no idea how his money was invested. He had spent more time researching his last laptop purchase than he had spent thinking about his retirement savings in the past decade.

'I suddenly realised,' he told me afterwards, 'that I had been treating the most important long-term financial decision of my life like a forgotten direct debit. I assumed it was fine. I had no evidence that it was fine. I had simply assumed.'

What unsettled Marcus was not that Linda had done better than him — he did not yet know whether she had. What unsettled him was that she had a plan, that she could articulate it, that she had made deliberate choices and could explain why she had made them. She was in control. Richard was also in control, in a different way — he had consciously delegated, having concluded that delegation was the right answer for his particular life. Marcus was simply absent from the equation.

Over the following 2 years, Marcus would research, consult, agonise, and ultimately make his own deliberate choice. His journey is, in many respects, the reason this book exists.

Three Paths, Three Kinds of Wisdom

The Self-Managed Super Fund (SMSF) literature — and there is a great deal of it — tends to present self-managed superannuation in one of two ways. Either it is a powerful wealth-building tool available to sophisticated investors willing to embrace its complexities and responsibilities. Or it is a regulatory minefield that destroys the retirement savings of people who underestimate what is involved.

Both are true. Neither is complete.

Linda, Marcus, and Richard represent three distinct but equally valid relationships with retirement savings, and this book is written for all three of them.

Linda represents the informed self-manager. She has the financial knowledge, the professional support network, the time discipline, and the genuine desire to be directly involved in her retirement investments. For her, an SMSF is not just a tax structure; it is an extension of the same professional competence she brings to everything else in her life. Her story shows what SMSF can achieve when it is used as it was designed to be used: as a powerful, flexible vehicle for building genuine wealth under the protection of a rigorous compliance framework.

Richard represents the informed delegator. He is not passive — he knows what he is paying for, monitors performance against benchmarks, and makes conscious decisions about when to stay and when to move. He has simply concluded, correctly for his circumstances, that the return on his time is higher in the operating theatre than at an investment desk. His story is a reminder that choosing not to have an SMSF is not a failure of sophistication. It is sometimes the most sophisticated choice of all.

Marcus represents the majority. He is educated, professionally successful, financially capable — but has never been given a clear picture of what SMSF actually is, what it actually costs, what it actually requires, and what it can actually achieve. His awakening at that dinner table is the awakening this book is trying to facilitate.

> **Who This Book Is For**
>
> This book is for you if you have ever looked at your superannuation statement and felt that vague unease — the sense that you should understand more than you do.
>
> It is for you if you have heard SMSF discussed at dinner parties or in professional circles and wondered whether it might be relevant to your situation.
>
> It is for you if you have an SMSF already, and are not entirely certain you understand the rules you are operating under.
>
> And it is for you if, like Richard, you have deliberately chosen to delegate — because understanding the landscape will make you a far more effective overseer of those to whom you have delegated.

What Happened in Between

Before explaining what this book is and how to use it, I want to tell you something about the 10 years that produced it.

Over those years, I have sat across from more than one hundred SMSF clients in an advisory capacity. Many of those meetings were the beginning of successful partnerships that have since delivered genuinely excellent outcomes. Some of those meetings, however, were crisis consultations — someone arriving at my office because something had gone wrong, or was about to, and they needed urgent help.

I have sat with James as he described watching his retirement savings depleted over 7 years of disability while he sat in a wheelchair and his family's financial life slowly unravelled around him — because he had decided that TPD insurance was an unnecessary expense, and he had been wrong.

I have helped Karen work through the implications of a single rent concession she made to her son's company — a $15,000-a-year gesture of family generosity — that triggered a tax liability of $191,250 and a permanent stain on her SMSF's tax record.

I watched Andrew — a senior partner at a law firm, a man who drafted contracts for a living — lose $180,000 in penalties, lost investment value, and compliance costs because he could not resist driving his 1967 Ford Mustang to a classic car exhibition.

I have sat with families in the weeks after a sudden death, trying to navigate the distribution of superannuation benefits through funds that had no binding death benefit nomination, and watched the results be simultaneously legally correct and personally devastating.

These stories are real. The numbers are real. The regret is real. I have changed names and some identifying details to protect the people involved, but the financial outcomes — the amounts lost, the fines imposed, the opportunities destroyed — are precisely as I have described them.

The total cost of the mistakes documented in this book exceeds $7.2 million. That is not a number I am proud of. It represents real damage to real people's retirement security, done — in almost every case —

not by bad actors but by well-meaning, intelligent, capable people who did not understand the rules they were operating under.

That ignorance is what this book exists to address.

A Candid Note on What This Book Cannot Do

Before we go any further, I need to be direct about something.

This book will give you a thorough understanding of how SMSFs work, what the rules are, where the dangers lie, and what good management looks like in practice. It will give you the pattern recognition to identify potential problems before they become expensive ones. It will make you a far more informed participant in conversations with financial advisers, accountants, and auditors.

What it cannot do — and what it is not designed to do — is qualify you to manage a superannuation fund without professional support.

The cases in this book include several where the person at the centre of the story was a lawyer, an accountant, a doctor, a financial professional. They were not ignorant of regulation in general. They were ignorant of the specific, technical, frequently counter-intuitive rules that govern SMSFs in particular. And that ignorance, in some cases, cost them hundreds of thousands of dollars.

The correct use of this book is as preparation. Read it to understand the landscape. Read it to know what questions to ask. Read it to recognise the warning signs when you encounter them. Then engage qualified professionals — an SMSF specialist financial adviser, a licensed SMSF auditor, an SMSF-experienced accountant — to translate that understanding into a strategy that is right for your specific circumstances.

> **$7,266,380 Total cost of mistakes documented in this book**

> Across 40 real case studies, spanning investment violations, tax penalties, insurance failures, estate planning disasters, and compliance breaches. Every dollar in this number was paid by a real person who thought they understood the rules.

The Structure of What Follows

This book follows the complete lifecycle of a self-managed superannuation fund. We begin with the fundamental question: should you establish one? We move through the structure of trustee responsibilities, the investment rules and their boundaries, the tax architecture, the insurance requirements, the contribution and withdrawal mechanics, the estate planning framework, and finally the winding-up process. Each chapter is built around real case studies, because I have found in 10 years of practice that people learn the rules best when they can see exactly what happens when those rules are broken.

Chapter One begins with two doctors who started from the same point in 2019 and arrived at outcomes $930,000 apart 5 years later. Their stories will frame everything that follows.

I hope, by the time you finish this book, that you will have the understanding Marcus gained — but without the 12 years of expensive ignorance that preceded it.

Paul Yang, CFP®

Sydney, 2025

Chapter One

Why This Book Exists

Two doctors. Identical starting points. A $930,000 gap after 5 years.

In the world of personal finance, we talk often about the power of compound interest — how small, consistent decisions accumulate over time into outcomes that seem, in retrospect, almost miraculous. What we discuss less frequently is the equal and opposite phenomenon: how a single structural decision, made without adequate information at the beginning of a process, compounds over years into a catastrophe that is almost impossible to reverse.

The story of Sarah and Michael is both of these things. It is a story about how good decisions compound into remarkable outcomes. And it is a story about how poor decisions — made not out of negligence, not out of greed, but simply out of insufficient understanding — can destroy a decade of accumulated wealth before anyone realises what is happening.

It is also the story that defines everything in this book. Every rule we will discuss, every case study we will examine, every warning we will sound finds its origin in some version of what happened between February 2019 and late 2024, when two people who started from exactly the same place arrived at outcomes separated by nearly a million dollars.

February 2019: Two Doctors, One Decision

Sarah and Michael had met at the University of Sydney Medical School in 1996. They had graduated together, completed their residencies at the same hospital, and established specialist practices in the same suburb of Sydney. Their careers had tracked each other closely for over 2 decades. By February 2019, both were 48 years old, both were earning approximately $380,000 a year, and both had accumulated roughly $700,000 in their superannuation accounts.

In the preceding months, both had come to the same conclusion independently: their money should be working harder. A retail superannuation fund, with no direct input from them, no ability to purchase specific assets, and no transparency about the investment decisions being made on their behalf, no longer felt adequate for the scale of wealth they were accumulating.

Both decided to establish a self-managed superannuation fund.

This is where their stories diverged.

Sarah's Decision: Investing in the Right Foundation

Sarah had always been methodical. It was what made her an excellent ophthalmologist — the ability to observe carefully, gather complete information, consider all the variables, and then act with precision. She applied the same methodology to her SMSF decision.

In January 2019, before she had done anything else, she called an SMSF specialist financial adviser. The initial consultation lasted 90 minutes, and she came prepared with questions she had written down in advance.

She asked about trustee responsibilities under the SIS Act. She asked about investment restrictions. She asked about the compliance obligations — the annual audit, the tax return, the investment strategy requirements. She asked about what she would need to do herself and what the adviser's firm would handle. She asked about the full cost structure, upfront and ongoing.

The adviser walked her through all of it, clearly and without condescension. By the end of that first meeting, Sarah had a clear picture of what she was taking on: the genuine control, the genuine responsibilities, and the genuine costs.

The adviser's recommendation: purchase a commercial property in Chatswood using a limited recourse borrowing arrangement (LRBA), while maintaining a diversified share and cash portfolio with the remaining funds. The commercial property would be leased to an unrelated third-party accounting firm at market rates. The LRBA would allow the SMSF to borrow $500,000 against the fund's $500,000 equity contribution to purchase a $1,000,000 property. This was precisely the kind of strategy that an SMSF could execute — one that was completely unavailable to her through a retail or industry fund.

Setup cost: $4,500. Annual operating costs: $3,700 (accounting $2,500, independent audit $1,200). Total first-year investment in professional infrastructure: $8,200.

Sarah committed. The SMSF was established in 6 weeks.

> **Sarah's Opening Investment Strategy (February 2019)**
>
> Commercial property (Chatswood): $1,000,000 via LRBA (SMSF equity $500,000, bank loan $500,000)
>
> Tenant: Unrelated third-party accounting firm at market rent of $68,000/year
>
> Vanguard ASX 200 ETF: $150,000
>
> Cash reserve (liquidity buffer): $50,000
>
> Written investment strategy: Filed, reviewed, and updated annually
>
> Sole Purpose Test compliance: Confirmed by adviser prior to purchase

Michael's Decision: The Allure of the Bargain

Michael was different. He was a gifted cardiologist and, like many high-achieving professionals, he carried a particular confidence about his ability to figure things out. He had navigated the complexity of medical school, specialist training, practice management, and property investment largely on his own terms. He was not inclined to pay for guidance he believed he could find more cheaply elsewhere.

In February 2019, he spent a Saturday afternoon researching SMSF establishment online. He found a package for $999 that included trust deed preparation, ATO registration, bank account setup, and a starter compliance kit. He purchased it that afternoon. His fund was registered within 48 hours.

For administration, he engaged his friend Mark, who had 'experience in banking and finance' and was willing to manage the fund's record-keeping for $800 a year. This arrangement saved Michael approximately $2,900 annually compared to professional management.

'I've saved $3,500 in setup fees,' Michael noted in a message to his wife. 'And I'm saving nearly $3,000 a year in management costs. This was the right call.'

He was calculating correctly. He simply wasn't calculating everything.

The Five-Year Chronicle: Sarah

Sarah's first year was straightforward and uneventful in the best possible way. The commercial property settled. The tenant — a ten-person accounting practice that had occupied the building for 3 years before the SMSF purchased it — continued paying $68,000 a year in rent. The Vanguard ETF returned 18.4% for the financial year ending June 2020, recovering strongly after the COVID-19 volatility. The cash reserve provided liquidity and peace of mind.

Sarah reviewed her investment strategy in January 2020 and updated it to reflect a planned rebalancing if the ETF position grew beyond 40% of the total portfolio. She attended the SMSF trustee education module her adviser recommended. She reviewed the annual audit results and signed off on the financial statements within 2 weeks of receiving them.

From a compliance perspective, her SMSF was a textbook example. From an investment perspective, it was performing exactly as planned.

The commercial property appreciated from $1,000,000 to $1,050,000 by June 2021, and to $1,100,000 by June 2022. The rental income of $68,000 a year was covering loan repayments of approximately $30,000 annually while contributing $38,000 net to the fund. The ETF holding of $150,000 had grown to $235,000 by June 2022 on the back of a strong equity bull market.

By June 2023, the property had been independently revalued at $1,150,000. Total rental income over 4 years: $272,000. Total loan repayments: $120,000. Net rental contribution to the fund: $152,000. The ETF had continued to grow, sitting at $262,000.

And then, in early 2024, Sarah's property manager called with news she had been quietly anticipating: the accounting firm tenant wanted to renew, and the market had moved. New rent: $76,000 a year. A 7% increase.

> **$1,350,000 Sarah's SMSF value at December 2024**
>
> Starting from $700,000 in February 2019. Commercial property net equity: $850,000 ($1.2M value minus $350,000 remaining loan). Shares: $280,000. Cash: $50,000. Accumulated net rental income: $170,000. Total five-year growth: $750,000 — a 120% return on initial capital.

Sarah's total investment in professional management over 5 years: $23,000 in advisory, accounting, and audit fees. Her total return over 5 years: $750,000.

The return on professional fees: 32 times the investment.

"The $23,000 I paid in professional fees over 5 years is the best investment I have ever made in my career. It is not even close." — Sarah

The Five-Year Chronicle: Michael

Michael's first few months went smoothly enough. Mark set up the bank accounts, registered the fund with the ATO, and provided Michael with a basic investment strategy template he found online. Michael reviewed it briefly and signed it.

In April 2019, Mark called with an investment opportunity.

'I have a friend in the tech space,' Mark explained. 'Company is about to go public. They need some pre-IPO equity investors. The upside is 5 times your money in 12 months. I can get you in for $200,000.'

Michael knew that pre-IPO investments in unlisted companies were high risk. He also knew that Mark had 'experience in banking.' He invested $200,000 of SMSF funds in the unlisted company.

In August 2019, Mark called again with another opportunity. A cryptocurrency trading platform with guaranteed returns of 15% annually. 'The algorithm is proprietary,' Mark explained. 'The returns are consistent. I've put my own money in.' Michael invested $150,000.

Then COVID arrived.

In March 2020, as markets collapsed, Mark panicked. He called Michael daily, recommending various defensive moves. On one particularly volatile day, he advised Michael to immediately liquidate the ETF component of the portfolio — $100,000 worth of shares that were now trading at around $65,000 following the market fall. Michael sold at the bottom, crystallising a $35,000 loss. Within 4 months, the market had recovered. Michael's $65,000 in cash had not participated in the recovery.

In June 2020, the unlisted technology company's IPO process collapsed. An investigation by the corporate regulator revealed that the business had significantly overstated its revenue. The company entered voluntary administration. Michael's $200,000 was gone.

In March 2021, the cryptocurrency platform suspended withdrawals. 3 months later, it shut down entirely. Regulatory investigations were announced in three countries. Michael's $150,000 was gone.

And that was before the ATO arrived.

The ATO Audit: When the Paperwork Catches Up

In May 2022, Michael received a letter from the Australian Taxation Office. The ATO had identified several areas of concern during a routine data-matching review and was requesting full documentation for the fund's 2019-20 and 2020-21 financial years.

Mark's record-keeping, it turned out, was not what Michael had imagined. Transaction records were incomplete. The investment strategy document, which had never been updated despite two major investment decisions, was inconsistent with the actual investments held. The fund's financial statements had been prepared 8 months late in 1 year, triggering an audit timing violation. The unlisted company shares, representing $200,000 at the time of purchase — fully 33% of the fund — had not been reviewed against the fund's investment strategy, which required diversification across at least four asset classes. A single unlisted entity at that concentration was directly inconsistent with the fund's own documented requirements.

The ATO's findings, delivered in September 2022, were comprehensive and devastating:

- Investment in the unlisted company was inconsistent with the fund's documented investment strategy, which required diversification across at least four asset classes: penalty of $6,600.
- Investment strategy not updated following the cryptocurrency investment: penalty of $6,600.

- Audit not completed within the required timeframe: penalty of $3,300.
- Failure to maintain adequate records per SIS Act requirements: penalty of $6,600.

Total administrative penalties: $23,100.

Michael hired a solicitor to respond to the ATO. The solicitor's fees over 12 months: $15,000.

In 2024, the ATO made a further determination. Based on the non-compliance findings, it declared the fund non-complying for the 2020-21 financial year. This triggered a back-taxation assessment at 45% on all undistributed income and assets at the beginning of that year. Total back-taxation: $42,000.

And then, in 2023, Mark's record-keeping problems became so extensive that the appointed auditor refused to sign off on the financial statements. Michael was forced to engage a professional accountant to reconstruct 3 years of financial records. Cost: $15,000.

$455,559 Michael's total five-year cost

Investment losses: $350,000 (unlisted company $200K + crypto $150K). ATO penalties: $28,560. Back-taxation: $42,000. Legal and remediation costs: $15,000 + $15,000. Mark's administration fees: $4,000. Initial setup: $999. Net SMSF value by December 2024: $420,000 — a loss of $280,000 on his original $700,000.

The Comparison: What a $930,000 Gap Looks Like

Measure	Sarah	Michael	Notes
Starting balance (Feb 2019)	$700,000	$700,000	Identical
Setup cost	$4,500	$999	Michael saved $3,501
5-year operating costs	$18,500	$4,000	Michael saved $14,500
Total 'savings' (Michael)	—	$18,000	The amount he was proud of
Investment losses	$0	$350,000	Two fraudulent schemes
ATO penalties	$0	$28,560	Compliance violations
Back-taxation	$0	$42,000	Non-complying year
Legal/remediation costs	$0	$30,000	Solicitor + reconstruction
SMSF value (Dec 2024)	$1,350,000	$420,000	The outcome
5-year growth rate	+120%	-30%	The gap: $930,000
Peace of mind	Complete	None	Priceless

To save $18,000 in professional fees, Michael incurred total losses of $455,559 in direct costs alone. His 'savings' cost him 25 times their value.

But that arithmetic understates the true cost. Because the real comparison is not between what Michael paid and what he saved. The real comparison is between where Michael ended up and where he could have ended up.

If Michael had left his $700,000 in a low-cost industry fund and achieved average market returns, he would have had approximately $1,000,000 by December 2024. If he had engaged professional SMSF management like Sarah, he would have had $1,350,000.

The gap between Michael's actual outcome ($420,000) and what professional management would have delivered ($1,350,000) is exactly $930,000.

That $930,000 is not just a number. It represents the difference between retiring at 62 with financial security and working until 68 out of necessity. It represents private school for Michael's children versus public school. It represents the holidays not taken, the experiences not had, the anxieties not resolved.

> **Michael's December 2024 Reflection**
>
> *"I thought I was saving money. I was actually destroying wealth.*
>
> *"I saved $18,000 in professional fees. I lost $455,559 in direct costs, and a further $160,001 in opportunity cost — money that could have been earning proper returns. Combined: $615,560, a ratio of 34 to 1.*
>
> *"If I could return to February 2019 with what I know now, I would write a cheque for 10 times Sarah's fees without hesitation. I would not think about it for a single second.*
>
> *"The thing nobody tells you is that SMSF is not a money-saving tool. It is a wealth-building tool. The professional*

> *fees are not a cost to be minimised — they are an investment in the infrastructure that makes everything else work. I had that exactly backwards."*

Understanding the Anatomy of the Difference

It would be tempting to conclude from Sarah and Michael's story that the lesson is simply: hire professionals. That is part of the lesson. But it is not the whole lesson.

The deeper lesson is structural. Sarah and Michael did not diverge because one was more intelligent than the other, or more financially capable, or more disciplined. They diverged because Sarah's framework had certain properties built into it from the beginning, and Michael's did not.

Property One: Professional Oversight

Sarah's adviser reviewed every significant investment decision before it was executed. This meant that no investment could be made that violated the fund's investment strategy, breached the SIS Act's prohibitions, or exposed the fund to disproportionate risk. When the Chatswood property opportunity was identified, the adviser performed due diligence on the tenant, the location, the valuation, the LRBA structure, and the compliance implications before any commitment was made.

Michael's framework had no equivalent filter. Mark was not qualified to assess investment compliance, had no professional indemnity insurance, and had no framework for evaluating whether a pre-IPO investment in an unlisted company was permissible under SMSF rules. He was, in effect, a bookkeeper attempting to perform the work of a financial adviser. The results were entirely predictable to anyone who understood the distinction.

Property Two: Written Strategy and Investment Discipline

Sarah's investment strategy was a living document. It was written by her adviser, reviewed annually, and updated whenever circumstances changed. It set out asset allocation ranges, liquidity requirements, and risk parameters. When the ETF grew beyond those parameters, the strategy flagged a rebalancing. When the property was revalued, the strategy was updated to reflect the new equity position.

Michael's investment strategy — such as it was — was a template document downloaded from the internet. It had not been updated following either the unlisted share investment or the cryptocurrency purchase. When the ATO reviewed the fund, they found that the fund's actual investments bore no meaningful relationship to the stated strategy. This is not a technical failing; it is a fundamental breach of the trustee's obligation to act in accordance with the fund's documented investment framework.

Property Three: Compliance Infrastructure

Sarah's fund had a licensed SMSF auditor appointed from day one. The auditor reviewed the fund's financial statements and compliance status annually, identified any potential issues early, and provided written confirmation that the fund had satisfied its obligations. This audit function is not optional — it is mandated by the SIS Act — but Sarah's adviser ensured it was performed properly and on time.

Michael's auditor was engaged through Mark's network and was inadequately experienced with the specific requirements of SMSF compliance. The audit was consistently late. The unlisted share breach — visible in the fund's own records — was not identified until the ATO's data-matching system flagged it more than 2 years after the breach occurred. By that time, the company had failed, the money was gone, and the ATO was on the doorstep.

Property Four: Access to Suitable Investments

The commercial property Sarah purchased was an investment type completely unavailable to her through a retail or industry fund. It generated $68,000 to $76,000 in annual rental income, provided capital appreciation of $300,000 over 5 years, and was structured through an LRBA that used the fund's leverage to amplify its equity returns. This is the genuine wealth-building power of an SMSF: the ability to access asset classes and structures that mainstream funds do not offer.

Michael's SMSF gave him access to exactly the same investment universe. He used it to invest in a fraudulent unlisted company and an insolvent cryptocurrency platform. The tool was not the problem. The absence of a qualified guide to help him use the tool correctly was the problem.

The $7,266,380: A Preview

Sarah and Michael's combined story accounts for $930,000 of the losses documented in this book. The remaining eight chapters contain 38 additional case studies, ranging from a $108,800 penalty for renting a holiday property to family members, to a $720,000 tax liability triggered by a single rent concession, to a $1,800,000 legal judgment that depleted an entire SMSF and required the owner to contribute personal savings to cover the shortfall.

In every single one of these cases, the person at the centre of the story was not reckless. They were not foolish. They were simply operating without a complete understanding of the rules. In some cases they had received advice and chosen not to follow it. In others, they had genuinely believed they understood the rules and had been wrong about something specific and technical.

The cumulative total across all 40 cases: $7,266,380.

This is your guidebook to avoiding every one of them.

Chapter	Subject	Key Cases	Total Lessons
2	Should You Have an SMSF?	Three 45-year-olds: $1.7M gap	Decision framework
3	Trustee Responsibilities	David & Robert: $250K court judgment	Three-layer duty system
4	Investment Rules	6 cases including $420K related party trap	$1,974,000
5	Tax Architecture	Jennifer: $191K NALI; Karen: $720K	$1,136,000
6	Insurance Strategy	James: $800K TPD; Emma: $1.8M liability	$2,600,000+
7	Contributions & Withdrawals	Steven's 28-day loss; Emily's in-specie error	$600,000+
8	Death Benefit Planning	Three family outcomes: Arthur, Patrick, Robert	Estate architecture
9	Winding Up	William's timing disaster; Patricia's CGT trap	$180,000+

How to Use This Book

Each chapter begins with a case study or series of case studies that make the stakes concrete. The technical content follows the human story, not the other way around. This is deliberate. In my experience, the rules stick in people's memories when they are anchored to specific consequences. You will remember the $191,250 cost of Jennifer's rent concession long after you have forgotten the section number of the relevant provision of the Income Tax Assessment Act.

At the end of each chapter, you will find a practical checklist that translates the chapter's lessons into concrete actions. These checklists are designed to be used in conversation with your adviser, not in isolation.

A note on the cases: all of the stories in this book are grounded in real events, real financial outcomes, and real regulatory actions. Names and some identifying details have been changed. Where cases are based on published court judgments, I have referenced the case citation. Where they are based on client experiences or published ATO decisions, I have characterised them as such.

- ☑ Use this book as preparation for professional conversations, not as a substitute for them.
- ☑ Read each case study carefully — the details matter, because the rules are extremely specific.
- ☑ Complete the chapter checklists before your next adviser meeting.
- ☐ Attempt to manage an SMSF based solely on what you read here.
- ☐ Assume that because you understand a principle, you can navigate the technical implementation without professional guidance.
- ☐ Forget Michael's story.

> **Sarah's Summary**
>
> *"This book showed me where the pitfalls were before I encountered them. Then I found a professional adviser and developed a strategy suited to my specific circumstances. The book gave me knowledge. The adviser gave me a plan. Together, they produced 5 years of $750,000 in growth.*
>
> *"Most importantly: the book helped me ask better questions. I walked into that first adviser meeting knowing what I wanted to understand, and that preparation made every subsequent conversation more productive.*
>
> *"Knowledge and professional guidance are not alternatives. They are partners."*

Turn to Chapter Two to begin the journey. We start with the most fundamental question: for you, specifically, is an SMSF the right answer?

The Psychology of the DIY Investor: Why Smart People Make Expensive Mistakes

There is a question I have asked myself many hundreds of times across my career, sitting across the table from clients who are clearly intelligent, often highly educated, and sometimes genuinely brilliant in their own professional domain — and who have nonetheless made catastrophically poor decisions with their superannuation. The question is not 'How could they not know?' The question is deeper: 'Why did they think they knew enough?'

The answer, I believe, has very little to do with financial literacy and everything to do with the cognitive architecture of human confidence. Psychologists call it the Dunning-Kruger effect — the well-documented phenomenon in which people with limited knowledge in a domain systematically overestimate their competence in that domain, while experts consistently underestimate theirs. In no field is this effect more reliably observed than in personal finance.

The individual who has successfully managed their own share portfolio for 5 years, or who has purchased and sold two investment properties, or who reads the financial pages every weekend — this person has accumulated genuine knowledge. What they have not accumulated is an accurate understanding of the boundaries of that knowledge. They know what they know. What they do not know is what they do not know. And in the highly regulated, technically complex environment of SMSF management, what you do not know can be ruinously expensive.

Michael, in our opening story, was not foolish. He was the exact opposite of foolish. He was a successful professional who had built substantial wealth through disciplined work and had taken a calculated risk on managing his retirement savings independently. His error was not in the calculation. It was in the calibration: he did not know enough to accurately assess the risk he was taking.

The Competence Gap: 6 Areas Where DIY Trustees Consistently Fall Short

After reviewing hundreds of SMSF cases over last decade, I have identified six specific domains where self-managed trustees — even capable, motivated ones — consistently underestimate the complexity and overestimate their own competence. These are not obscure regulatory niches. They are the core operational requirements of SMSF management. And failing in any one of them can produce a disproportionately large financial loss.

Competence Domain	What DIY Trustees Typically Know	What They Often Don't Know
Related Party Rules	Cannot buy property from	Definition of 'related party' extends to companies they

	family at below-market rates	control; intermediary structures don't help; NALI applies to non-arm's length expenses too
Contribution Timing	There are annual contribution caps	Settlement date ≠ allocation date (TD 2013/22); work test applies 67–74 for deductible contributions only (not NCCs); catch-up rules; TSB thresholds change the caps available
Investment Strategy	Must have a written strategy	Strategy must be reviewed when circumstances change; must specifically address insurance; must be specific enough to justify actual holdings
Pension Rules	Must draw minimum pension each year	Minimum percentage changes by age; failure loses ECPI for entire year; commutation requirements at wind-up
Death Benefits	Can nominate beneficiary	Nominations lapse; non-lapsing options depend on deed;

		proportional rule affects tax; LPR nomination differs from direct beneficiary
Tax Architecture	Fund pays 15% tax	ECPI method choices; NALI contamination is permanent; franking credit optimisation; CGT discount timing

The gap between what DIY trustees typically know and what the competent management of an SMSF actually requires is not small. It is the difference between knowing that a motor vehicle has an engine, and knowing how to maintain that engine across 200,000 kilometres of varied road conditions. One produces correct answers on a knowledge test. The other produces outcomes.

The Five Psychological Traps of Self-Managed Investing

Beyond the knowledge gap, there are specific psychological dynamics that reliably lead SMSF trustees astray. Understanding them is not a guarantee of avoiding them — humans are not saved from cognitive biases simply by being aware of them. But awareness does increase the likelihood of catching yourself in the trap before the damage is done.

Trap One: Overconfidence from Recent Success

The year before Michael made his worst investment decisions was, by his own account, one of his best years as an investor. He had identified a lithium stock early, sold at the right time, and netted approximately $85,000 on a $40,000 investment. He had 'a feel for it.' The confidence that followed that success was perfectly understandable — and perfectly misplaced. A single good outcome in a favourable market environment tells you almost nothing about your ability to consistently outperform. But the emotional experience of that win produces a genuine, biochemical sensation of competence that is extremely difficult to override with rational analysis.

Trap Two: Loss Aversion and the Doubled-Down Position

When Michael's first alternative asset — the unlisted company — began to decline, his rational response would have been to exit and accept the loss. The emotional response, which is to say the human response, was to assume the decline was temporary and to view the falling price as a buying opportunity. He did not buy more — but he held far longer than a dispassionate assessment would have justified, because selling meant crystallising the loss and acknowledging the mistake. The same dynamic played out with the cryptocurrency position. By the time he sold, both had lost the majority of their value. The emotional cost of admitting error had made the financial cost dramatically larger.

Trap Three: The Narrative Fallacy

Every bad investment has a compelling story. The unlisted company Michael invested in had excellent management, a genuinely innovative product, and three independent analysts' endorsements. The cryptocurrency had a transformative technology thesis that, stripped of the speculative overlay, was not entirely implausible. Stories are cognitively compelling. Returns are arithmetically indifferent to them. The narrative fallacy — our tendency to construct a causal explanation that makes the investment feel inevitable — is the single most reliable predictor of retail investor underperformance that I have encountered in the academic literature and in my own practice.

Trap Four: The Authority Substitution

Michael's administrator, his friend Mark, was not an SMSF specialist. He was a general accountant who happened to be available and cheap. Michael trusted him not because of his documented expertise in superannuation compliance, but because of the pre-existing relationship. This trust substituted for the due diligence that would have revealed — quickly — that Mark lacked the specific qualifications and knowledge to protect Michael from the regulatory risks he was accumulating. When selecting professional advisers for your SMSF, the relevant question is not 'Do I trust this person?' It is 'Does this person have the specific, current, documented expertise that this function requires?'

Trap Five: The Complexity Illusion

There is a specific cognitive error that highly intelligent people are particularly prone to: confusing the ability to understand a concept when explained with the ability to implement it correctly across all relevant circumstances. Michael could understand the in-house asset rules when they were explained to him. He could understand the sole purpose test. He could understand the arm's length requirement for related party transactions. What he could not do — because it requires years of practice-based experience, not just conceptual understanding — was apply those rules in real time to the specific, ambiguous, edge-case circumstances that real SMSF management constantly produces. Intelligence is necessary but not sufficient. Expertise requires practice.

The Cost of Getting It Wrong: Beyond the Dollar Figure

The $930,000 gap between Sarah and Michael at the five-year mark is, in purely financial terms, the central quantitative fact of Chapter One. But I want to dwell for a moment on the costs that don't appear in the comparison table, because they are in many ways the costs that matter most to the people who experience them.

When I spoke with Michael — a composite of several real clients, but closely drawn from life — he described the 18 months following the ATO audit as the most stressful of his professional career. The combination of the financial losses, the regulatory penalties, and the administrative burden of remediation consumed approximately three hundred hours of his time and a sustained level of cognitive load that interfered with his ability to perform in his actual profession. He took 3 days off during the audit process. He estimated, conservatively, that his performance at work during that period was operating at about 70% of normal capacity.

He also described the social and personal cost: the conversations with his wife that he had dreaded, the decision not to tell his adult children about the full extent of the losses until the remediation was complete, the persistent feeling that he had let his family down. These costs are not quantifiable in a comparison table. But they are real. And they are, in my experience, the most lasting consequence of an SMSF that has gone wrong — not the loss of money, which can be partially recovered, but the loss of confidence and the tax on relationships that financial stress reliably produces.

Sarah, by contrast, described her investment experience over the same five-year period with the particular satisfaction of someone who had made a plan, executed it well, and watched it produce results. She was not complacent — she checked her portfolio quarterly, had an annual review with her financial planner, and had made three strategy adjustments in response to changing market conditions. But the psychological experience of the process was one of managed engagement, not crisis management. Her SMSF was, in her words, 'working for me, not against me.'

The 3 Questions Every SMSF Trustee Should Ask Each Year

1. Are all my compliance obligations met for this financial year — contributions, minimum pension, audit, annual return? 2. Is my investment strategy current and connected to my actual holdings — including a specific assessment of insurance coverage? 3. Is my death benefit planning up to date — BDBN valid and current, reversionary pension nominated, will aligned with superannuation intentions? A 'yes' to all three does not guarantee a perfect outcome. A 'no' to any one of them is a signal that requires immediate attention.

A Note on How to Use This Book

This is not a book designed to be read once and placed on a shelf. It is a reference document — a working companion to your ongoing relationship with your SMSF. The most useful approach I can suggest: read it through once to build the overall framework, then return to the specific chapters most relevant to your current situation and life stage.

If you are approaching 65, Chapter Seven on contributions is immediately actionable. If you have a commercial property in your SMSF, Chapter Four on investment rules will repay rereading. If you have adult children who are not financially dependent on you, Chapter Eight on death benefits contains planning insights worth revisiting with your adviser.

The appendices — the establishment checklist, the annual compliance calendar, the glossary, and the questions to ask your adviser — are designed as practical working tools. Copy them, mark them, use them in your annual review meeting. They represent the distilled operational knowledge of 2 decades of practice, compressed into formats that you can act on immediately.

Now, let us turn to the foundational question: is an SMSF actually the right structure for your specific situation?

Chapter Two
Is an SMSF Right for You?

Three professionals. The same starting balance. A $2.97 million gap after 10 years.

Before we discuss a single investment rule or tax provision, we need to address the most important question in this book: should you establish a self-managed superannuation fund at all?

This is not a question with a universal answer. The SMSF literature — and the industry that supports it — has a built-in tendency toward optimism about the virtues of self-management. Advisers who specialise in SMSFs, accountants who service them, and lawyers who draft their trust deeds all have structural incentives to recommend them. I want to be direct about that bias, including my own.

An SMSF is the right answer for some people, in some circumstances, with some level of commitment. It is emphatically not the right answer for everyone, and the consequences of getting this decision wrong — of establishing an SMSF when a well-managed industry fund would have served you better, or of establishing one without adequate professional support — can be severe.

This chapter will give you the honest framework for making that decision.

Three Professionals, Three Choices: The Ten-Year Projection

To understand the stakes involved in this decision, let us begin with three professionals who found themselves at the same decision point in 2024. All three were 45 years old. All three had superannuation balances of $500,000. All three were asking the same question: what should I do?

Their names are Michael, Sarah, and David. (Different people from Chapter One — common names, common stories.) 10 years later, in 2044, their retirement accounts will reflect the consequences of the choices they are about to make.

Michael: The Path of Convenience

Michael is a software engineer who has built a successful career at a large technology company. He is intelligent, busy, and financially comfortable. He has never found superannuation particularly interesting, and he does not expect that to change. His existing retail fund — a large, well-known super fund — has served him adequately. The annual management fee of 0.85% feels invisible. The balanced investment option has delivered reasonable returns.

Michael decides to stay where he is. He makes no changes.

Over the next 10 years, his $500,000 will be subject to a management fee that, as his balance grows, also grows in absolute dollar terms. In 2024, the fee is $4,250. By 2034, as his balance reaches $900,000, the fee has grown to $7,650. By 2044, it is nearly $12,000 a year. Over 10 years, the cumulative fee impact — in both dollars paid and compound growth lost — is approximately $130,000.

His 2044 balance: $1,850,000. Annual sustainable retirement income at 7%: $129,500.

This is a good outcome. Michael will retire comfortably. He paid nothing in professional fees beyond his management charges. He never worried about compliance.

Sarah: The Path of Optimisation Within Constraints

Sarah is a general practitioner who has always been careful with money. She has researched industry funds and concluded that her current retail fund, at 0.85%, is overcharging her. She switches to a well-regarded industry fund charging 0.45%.

Over 10 years, this single decision saves her approximately $60,000 in fees compared to Michael's retail fund. Her fund's investment returns are slightly better than Michael's, reflecting the industry fund's lower cost structure and diversified portfolio. She makes no additional decisions. She is on the high-growth investment option and leaves it there.

Her 2044 balance: $2,150,000. Annual sustainable retirement income: $150,500.

Sarah has done better than Michael with a single low-effort decision. She, too, will retire comfortably.

David: The Path of Deliberate Control

David is an accountant. He understands financial structures, tax law, and compound returns. He has been planning this decision for 3 years. He engages an SMSF specialist financial adviser in early 2024.

David's strategy: establish an SMSF and use a Limited Recourse Borrowing Arrangement to purchase an $800,000 commercial property in a logistics precinct in Western Sydney. He contributes $300,000 of fund equity and arranges a $500,000 bank loan through the SMSF structure. The remaining $200,000 goes into a diversified share portfolio — Australian and international ETFs.

The commercial property is leased to an unrelated logistics company at a market rent of $60,000 per year. Loan repayments are $38,000 per year. Net rental contribution: $22,000 annually.

David's SMSF costs $4,500 per year to run: accounting, audit, ASIC registration, and professional advisory fees. These costs are fixed regardless of how large his balance grows.

The investment strategy is reviewed annually. When David reaches60, he transitions the fund to pension phase. All investment income — rent, dividends, capital gains — becomes entirely tax-free.

Year	Property Value	Shares Value	Annual Rent Net	Total Assets

2024	$800,000	$200,000	$22,000	$500,000 (starting equity)
2029	$990,000	$280,000	$24,000	$780,000
2034	$1,220,000	$395,000	$28,000	$1,200,000
2039	$1,500,000	$555,000	$32,000	$1,850,000
2044	$1,850,000	$680,000	$38,000	$3,550,000

David's 2044 balance: $3,550,000. Annual sustainable retirement income at 7%: $248,500.

The gap between David and Michael: $1,700,000.

The gap between David and Sarah: $1,400,000.

> **The Tax Multiplier**
>
> One reason David's outcome diverges so dramatically from Michael's and Sarah's is the tax advantage of pension phase.
>
> David's $60,000 annual rental income in pension phase: $0 tax.
>
> The same $60,000 in a personal account (taxed at 37%): $22,200 tax every year.
>
> Over 10 years of pension phase, David saves approximately $444,000 in tax on rental income alone.
>
> This is before accounting for dividend income, capital gains on share sales, and the eventual CGT-free disposal of the property.
>
> The tax advantage of superannuation in pension phase is the most powerful wealth-building mechanism available to

> Australian investors. An SMSF unlocks the ability to direct that mechanism toward specific, high-quality assets.

But Consider Tom: The Fourth Path

Tom is also 55, also has $500,000, and also establishes an SMSF in 2024. But Tom takes the Michael approach from Chapter One: he does it himself, he cuts professional fees to zero, and he relies on his own judgment and a friend's tips.

Tom's ten-year outcome: $580,000. A thirty-year working career of compulsory contributions, and he ends up with less than he started.

The gap between David and Tom: $2,970,000.

Tom will not retire at65. He will work until his health prevents him from working, at which point he will rely on the Age Pension.

Measure	Michael (Retail)	Sarah (Industry)	David (SMSF)	Tom (DIY SMSF)
2044 Balance	$1,850,000	$2,150,000	$3,550,000	$580,000
20-Year Fees	$130,000	$70,000	$90,000	$nil (+ $1.4M in losses)
Annual Income	$129,500	$150,500	$248,500	$40,600
Investment Control	Low	Low	Complete	Unlimited (but poorly used)
Compliance Status	Zero risk	Zero risk	Fully compliant	Multiple breaches

Mental State 2044	Comfortable	Comfortable	Financially free	Working or dependent

What Exactly Is an SMSF? Three Identities, One Structure

The phrase 'self-managed superannuation fund' is slightly misleading, because it emphasises the 'self-managed' component at the expense of the two more foundational elements. Before making any decision about whether an SMSF is right for you, you need to understand what it actually is — not just the self-management part, but all three of its legal identities.

Identity One: A Trust Structure

At its legal foundation, an SMSF is a trust. It has trustees (the people who manage it), beneficiaries (the members, who are usually the same people as the trustees), and trust property (the fund's assets). This trust structure is not a technicality — it has real and significant consequences.

The most important of these consequences is protection. Because the SMSF's assets are held by the trust, not by the individual members, they are legally distinct from the members' personal assets. Creditors of an SMSF member generally cannot access the fund's assets to satisfy personal debts.

> **Andrew's Bankruptcy: Trust Protection in Practice**
>
> In 2023, Andrew's personal business failed with debts of $2 million. His creditors included suppliers, employees, and the ATO.
>
> Andrew's personal bank account: $50,000 — frozen immediately.

> Andrew's personal investment property: $800,000 — sold under a court order to partially satisfy debts.
>
> Andrew's SMSF: $1,500,000 — completely protected.
>
> The bankruptcy trustee confirmed in court: 'Mr Andrew's SMSF is an independent trust entity. It does not form part of the bankrupt estate.'
>
> Andrew retained his entire superannuation and retired on schedule at 65 with $1.5 million intact.
>
> Important caveat: This protection applies to legitimately accumulated funds. Transfers designed to shelter assets from existing creditors, or contributions made in anticipation of bankruptcy, are subject to clawback provisions.

The trust structure also imposes obligations. As a trustee, you are not the owner of the SMSF's assets in any ordinary sense — you are their legal custodian, obligated to manage them for the benefit of the fund's members in accordance with the trust deed and the law. This distinction matters enormously, as we will see in Chapter Three.

Identity Two: A Superannuation Fund

An SMSF is also a regulated superannuation fund, governed by the Superannuation Industry (Supervision) Act 1993 — universally known as the SIS Act. This regulatory status is what gives the fund access to the superannuation tax concessions: a 15% tax rate on investment income and contributions during the accumulation phase, and 0% tax rate on income and gains once the fund is paying retirement pensions.

It is also what imposes the compliance obligations. The ATO regulates SMSFs directly — unlike large retail and industry funds, which are regulated by the Australian Prudential Regulation Authority (APRA), SMSFs fall under ATO jurisdiction, which means the ATO has direct visibility into each fund's tax return, investment records, and compliance history.

The regulatory architecture includes mandatory annual audits by an approved SMSF auditor, annual tax returns, and an investment strategy requirement. It also includes a comprehensive set of investment prohibitions — the 'rules of what you cannot do' — that are the subject of Chapter Four.

The consequences of non-compliance range from administrative penalties (typically between $6,600 and $19,800 per breach) to the catastrophic designation of the fund as 'non-complying,' which subjects the entire fund's assets to a 45% tax rate. This is, in effect, the financial equivalent of a nuclear detonation within your retirement savings.

Identity Three: Self-Managed

The self-management component means that you — as trustee — are responsible for all investment decisions. You decide what to buy, when to buy it, when to sell, how to structure the portfolio, and how to balance competing objectives. This is genuine, substantive control.

It is also genuine, substantive responsibility. Everything that goes wrong in the fund is your responsibility as trustee, regardless of who provided the advice or executed the trade. The ATO does not accept 'my accountant told me to' as a defence to a trustee breach. Professional advisers can be found jointly and severally liable, but the trustee liability does not disappear.

The self-management identity is the double-edged sword that makes this entire discussion necessary. Used well, it is a powerful wealth-building capability. Used badly, it is a mechanism for destroying decades of accumulated wealth with extraordinary efficiency.

The Four Essential Conditions

An SMSF must satisfy 4 conditions to be a validly regulated superannuation fund:

1. Members cannot exceed six. SMSFs are by definition small, private funds. Most have between one and 4 members, typically a couple or a couple plus adult children.
2. Each member must be a trustee (or director of the corporate trustee). This is the 'self-managed' component made concrete — you cannot be a member without being a trustee.
3. The fund must satisfy the Sole Purpose Test — it must be maintained solely for the purpose of providing retirement benefits to members, or death benefits to beneficiaries. We will examine this in detail in Chapter Three.
4. The fund must comply with the investment rules of the SIS Act — the prohibitions on borrowing, lending, and related-party transactions that form the subject of Chapter Four.

Corporate trustees — a private company established specifically to act as trustee — are strongly preferred over individual trustees by most SMSF advisers, despite the modest additional cost. The reasons are practical: a corporate trustee simplifies the administration of member changes (adding or removing members does not require re-registering assets), provides an additional layer of limited liability protection, and generally produces cleaner, more professionally structured funds.

The Cost Analysis: When SMSF Makes Financial Sense

The most common question I receive from people considering an SMSF is: 'Is it worth it financially?' The answer, like most answers in financial planning, is: it depends.

The key variable is the relationship between your fund's balance and the fees you are currently paying. Retail and industry fund fees are percentage-based. SMSF operating costs are largely fixed. This creates a mathematical breakeven point that is fundamental to the decision.

Balance	Retail Fund (0.85%)	Industry Fund (0.45%)	SMSF (~$4,500)	SMSF Advantage vs Industry
$200,000	$1,700/yr	$900/yr	$4,500/yr	SMSF more expensive by $3,600
$350,000	$2,975/yr	$1,575/yr	$4,500/yr	SMSF more expensive by $2,925
$500,000	$4,250/yr	$2,250/yr	$4,500/yr	Roughly breakeven vs industry
$750,000	$6,375/yr	$3,375/yr	$4,500/yr	SMSF saves $1,125 vs industry
$1,000,000	$8,500/yr	$4,500/yr	$4,500/yr	SMSF equal to industry
$1,500,000	$12,750/yr	$6,750/yr	$4,500/yr	SMSF saves $2,250 vs industry
$2,000,000	$17,000/yr	$9,000/yr	$4,500/yr	SMSF saves $4,500 vs industry

The commonly cited threshold for SMSF cost-effectiveness is approximately $200,000 to $300,000. Below this level, SMSF operating costs are disproportionately high relative to the fund's assets. Above $500,000, an SMSF begins to be competitive with industry funds on pure cost grounds. Above $1,000,000, it is clearly more cost-efficient than any percentage-based fee structure.

But the fee comparison is not the whole story. For David, the primary financial argument for his SMSF was not the fee saving — it was the access to assets and strategies that generated a $3,550,000 outcome instead of a $2,150,000 outcome. The $90,000 he paid in SMSF costs over 10 years was not a cost to be minimised; it was an investment infrastructure that enabled a $1,400,000 incremental outcome over the best available alternative.

Emma's Real Saving: The Fee Advantage in Practice

Emma established an SMSF in 2020 with a $1.5 million account. She had previously been paying 0.85% annually in a well-known retail fund.

Her SMSF operating cost: $4,500 per year.

What she would have paid in the retail fund (5 years, accounting for balance growth): approximately $70,000.

What she actually paid in SMSF fees (5 years): $22,500.

Fee saving: $47,500.

Emma's comment: 'That $47,500 became the deposit on the commercial property my SMSF now holds. The fee saving created the investment opportunity.'

The Decision Framework: 4 Questions

After reviewing hundreds of SMSF decisions over ten years, I have distilled the decision into 4 questions. If you can answer all four affirmatively, an SMSF is likely worth serious exploration. If you answer any of them negatively, either the timing is wrong or the structure is not right for your circumstances.

Question One: Is Your Balance Large Enough?

The general threshold is $200,000, but in practice, I recommend waiting until $300,000 to $400,000 before establishing an SMSF. At $200,000, the operating cost of $4,500 represents a 2.25% drag on your balance — worse than almost any retail fund's management fee. At $400,000, that same $4,500 is 1.125%. At $600,000, it is 0.75% — already comparable with, or better than, many retail funds.

The exception is when the investment strategy involves assets that generate substantially higher returns than a standard managed fund could achieve. If David's commercial property generates effective returns of 12% annually compared to the 7% available through an industry fund, the fee comparison becomes less important — the strategy itself justifies the structure.

Question Two: Do You Have Access to Professional Support?

This is the question that determines whether an SMSF becomes David's story or Tom's. An SMSF without professional support is not an SMSF operating at reduced cost. It is an SMSF operating under substantially elevated risk of regulatory failure, investment mistake, and ultimately catastrophic loss.

The professional team you need: an SMSF specialist financial adviser (to advise on investment strategy, tax planning, and lifecycle decisions), an SMSF-experienced accountant (to prepare the annual financial statements and tax return), and a licensed SMSF auditor (to provide the mandatory independent audit). In many cases, one firm will provide all three. In others, you will have separate relationships.

Cost: approximately $3,000 to $10,000 per year depending on complexity. This is not optional. It is the foundational infrastructure without which the entire structure is at risk.

Question Three: Are You Willing to Be Genuinely Engaged?

Even with professional support, being an SMSF trustee requires active engagement. You will need to review and sign off on the annual financial statements, update your investment strategy when circumstances change, understand the basis for each investment decision, and remain aware of any compliance obligations that require your attention.

The minimum commitment for a well-run SMSF is approximately fifteen to ten-5 hours per year. This is not a massive time commitment for most professionals, but it is a real one. Linda spends ten-five to 30 hours annually on her SMSF — reviewing her investment strategy, attending meetings with her adviser, reviewing the audit results. She considers this time well spent. If the idea of spending ten-5 hours a year on your retirement finances feels burdensome rather than appropriate, an SMSF may not be right for you at this point in your life.

Question Four: Do You Understand the Sole Purpose Test?

This might seem like an unusual question to include in a high-level decision framework, but I have seen too many SMSFs established by people who fundamentally misunderstood its most basic rule to omit it.

The Sole Purpose Test requires that an SMSF be maintained solely for the purpose of providing retirement benefits. Not primarily — solely. This means no personal use of the fund's assets, no investments designed to benefit related parties, no transactions structured to provide current benefits to members or their families. These restrictions are absolute and strictly enforced.

If you are considering an SMSF because you want to invest in a holiday property you can occasionally use, or because you want to loan money to your business, or because you want to provide your children with affordable housing — stop. These arrangements are prohibited, often severely penalised, and will almost certainly cost you more than any benefit they provide. We will examine these rules in detail in Chapter Three and Four.

> **The Decision Checklist**
>
> Consider an SMSF if ALL of the following apply:
>
> ✓ Superannuation balance above $200,000 (ideally $400,000+)
>
> ✓ Access to qualified SMSF specialist adviser, accountant, and auditor
>
> ✓ Prepared to spend 15-25 hours annually on fund management
>
> ✓ A specific investment strategy in mind that is genuinely better than alternatives
>
> ✓ Clear understanding that the fund's assets cannot benefit you personally
>
> ✗ Do NOT consider an SMSF if:
>
> ✗ Balance below $200,000 (fees will exceed benefits)
>
> ✗ No access to or interest in professional support
>
> ✗ Want a 'set and forget' solution
>
> ✗ Primary motivation is to invest in assets you intend to use personally
>
> ✗ You have no financial knowledge and no interest in developing any

The Regulatory Landscape: Who Is Watching

Before leaving this chapter, it is worth understanding the regulatory context within which SMSFs operate. Unlike APRA-regulated funds (retail and industry funds), SMSFs are regulated directly by the Australian Taxation Office. This has important practical implications.

The ATO receives the SMSF's annual tax return and audit report. It cross-matches this data against other information sources — property records, ASIC registers, bank data, and third-party reports. Its data-matching capability has improved dramatically over the past decade. Transactions that might once have gone unnoticed — below-market rent to related parties, undisclosed personal use of fund assets, unreported related-party transactions — are increasingly detectable through data analytics.

The ATO's compliance posture toward SMSFs has also hardened. In the 3 years from 2021 to 2023, the ATO issued more than $186 million in SMSF penalties and back-taxes, up from $98 million in the preceding 3 years. The lesson: the days when an SMSF operated under genuine regulatory invisibility are over. Every trust deed, every tax return, every audit report is potentially subject to scrutiny.

This is not a reason to avoid an SMSF. It is a reason to run one properly.

Chapter Two Summary: The Core Questions

By the end of this chapter, you should have a clear framework for answering the fundamental SMSF question: is it right for you?

> **5 Things This Chapter Has Established**
>
> 1. The financial advantage of a well-run SMSF over retail and industry funds can exceed $1.4 million over 10 years — but only with professional management.
>
> 2. A poorly run SMSF can produce outcomes dramatically worse than any managed fund alternative. The gap between David and Tom in our scenario was $2.97 million.
>
> 3. The financial breakeven point for SMSF cost-effectiveness is approximately $300,000 to $500,000, depending on the comparison fund and the specific SMSF strategy.

> 4. The decision to establish an SMSF requires a commitment to ongoing professional support, annual engagement, and strict compliance with investment rules.
>
> 5. The self-management component is the source of both the opportunity and the risk. The outcome depends entirely on how that self-management capability is exercised.

In Chapter Three, we turn to what is perhaps the most misunderstood aspect of SMSF trusteeship: the weight of legal responsibility that comes with the role, and the very real consequences — measured in hundreds of thousands of dollars — that follow from misunderstanding it.

The Three Archetypes of SMSF Trustees: Which One Are You?

In a decade of SMSF practice, I have observed three distinct archetypes of trustee — three fundamentally different relationships that individuals have with the concept of managing their own retirement savings. Understanding which archetype you most closely resemble is not merely an intellectual exercise. It is a practical assessment that should inform every decision you make about your SMSF, from whether to establish one at all, to how much professional support to seek, to what investment strategy is most appropriate for your temperament and available time.

Archetype One: The Engaged Director

The Engaged Director treats their SMSF as a genuine fiduciary responsibility — a legal obligation that requires competence, ongoing education, and systematic compliance attention. They read the ATO's SMSF newsletters. They attend their annual review meetings prepared with specific questions. They understand their investment strategy, can explain it to a stranger, and update it when circumstances change. They view their auditor not as an adversary but as a quality-control mechanism for their own governance.

The Engaged Director typically falls into one of two sub-types. The first is the investment-focused type: a person with genuine interest in financial markets, investment strategy, and portfolio construction, who values the SMSF primarily for the investment control and flexibility it provides. The second is the tax-architecture type: a person primarily interested in the tax efficiency of the structure, who invests in competent professional support and focuses their own energy on strategic decision-making rather than investment selection.

Both sub-types of the Engaged Director tend to produce excellent outcomes from their SMSFs. Their engagement is the primary driver of those outcomes — not the intelligence of their investment strategy, not the sophistication of their tax planning, but the discipline of ongoing attention and the willingness to seek and apply expert advice when their own knowledge reaches its limits.

Archetype Two: The Passive Holder

The Passive Holder established their SMSF for a specific reason — typically to purchase a direct property or to consolidate a large superannuation balance — and has since largely delegated its management to a professional adviser or accountant. They review their annual statements, sign whatever documents their adviser sends, and generally trust that compliance is being managed appropriately.

The Passive Holder is not negligent. They are trusting — and in most cases, their trust is reasonably well-placed. The risk profile of the Passive Holder is specific: they are exposed to the errors and omissions of the professionals they have delegated to, without the personal oversight that would catch those errors early. A competent, specialist adviser mitigates this risk substantially. A generalist accountant who also happens to provide SMSF compliance services may not.

If you recognise yourself as a Passive Holder, the specific action I recommend is an independent second-opinion review of your SMSF's compliance status every three to 5 years. Not a replacement of your current adviser, but a validation exercise — engage a different specialist to review the fund's files and confirm that everything is in order. The cost is a few thousand dollars. The peace of mind, and the occasional discovery of something that needs to be addressed, is consistently worth it.

Archetype Three: The Reluctant Administrator

The Reluctant Administrator is, in my experience, the most common and the most concerning of the three archetypes. They established their SMSF with good intentions and perhaps genuine enthusiasm — attracted by the control narrative, the property investment opportunity, or a specific tax strategy. But over time, the administrative burden has grown to exceed their willingness to engage with it. They sign documents without reading them. They defer compliance discussions. They have not reviewed their investment strategy in 3 years. They are vaguely aware that their BDBN may have lapsed but have not gotten around to addressing it.

The Reluctant Administrator is not a bad person or a bad investor. They are a person whose specific circumstances — typically a combination of professional busyness, genuine complexity aversion, and the absence of a clear trigger to re-engage — have produced a gap between the legal obligations they accepted when they became trustees and the level of engagement they are actually able to sustain.

The honest question for the Reluctant Administrator is whether to recommit to the engagement the SMSF requires — by restructuring the professional support, building better systems, and making compliance a priority — or whether to accept that the SMSF structure is not appropriate for their current life stage and plan an orderly transition to a retail or industry fund. Both answers are legitimate. The dangerous answer is to do neither: to continue as a Reluctant Administrator, accumulating compliance risk while maintaining the fiction of active management.

The balance threshold question is most relevant for members whose intended use of the SMSF is broadly equivalent to what a low-cost retail or industry fund would provide. If you are primarily seeking a low-cost, diversified, well-governed investment vehicle for accumulating retirement savings, and you do not have specific investment, tax, or estate planning reasons to require a self-managed structure, the balance threshold matters significantly. If you have compelling reasons to require a self-managed structure, the balance threshold is a secondary consideration.

The LRBA as SMSF Catalyst: Evaluating Property-Driven Establishment

The most common reason members establish an SMSF — by a substantial margin — is to borrow to purchase a direct property through a limited recourse borrowing arrangement. The LRBA is both the most powerful and the most risky feature of the SMSF structure, and evaluating whether it is appropriate for your specific situation requires a clear-eyed assessment of multiple factors that most real estate promoters will not raise in their marketing materials.

What the LRBA Actually Costs

When an SMSF borrows to purchase a property, the effective cost of the investment is not simply the purchase price. It includes: the deposit, which must come from existing SMSF assets (typically a minimum of 10% to 30% of the purchase price); borrowing costs (establishment fees, ongoing interest, exit fees); the holding trust structure (legal costs to establish the bare trust / holding trust required by the LRBA structure); ongoing property costs (management fees, maintenance, insurance, rates); and the opportunity cost of the deposit amount, which is committed to the property and unavailable for diversification.

The interest rate on an SMSF LRBA is typically higher than an owner-occupier home loan rate, because the lender's recourse is limited to the acquired property. In a period of high interest rates — as Australia experienced from 2022 to 2025 — SMSF LRBA interest rates of seven to 8% are not uncommon. At 8% interest on a $600,000 loan, the fund is paying $48,000 per year in interest before the property produces any net return.

The Rental Yield Reality Check

Many members who pursue SMSF LRBA strategies are attracted by the combination of capital growth potential and rental income. The capital growth argument is long-term and speculative — property values do rise over time in most Australian markets, but the timing and quantum of that growth is uncertain. The rental income argument is more immediate, but requires a realistic assessment.

For commercial property — the preferred SMSF property type because of the business real property related-party rules — gross rental yields of five to 8% are achievable in many markets. But the net yield, after property management fees (typically six to 10%of gross rent), maintenance, insurance, vacancy periods, and other holding costs, is typically one to two percentage points lower. Against an LRBA interest rate of seven to 8%, a net yield of four to 6% means that the property is cash-flow negative — the fund must find additional cash (from contributions or other income) to service the interest shortfall.

This is not an argument against SMSF property investment. It is an argument for doing the arithmetic honestly, with a realistic assessment of rental yields and vacancy periods, before committing the fund to a multi-decade borrowing obligation. The members who do this arithmetic and still proceed, because they are convinced of the long-term capital growth case and can sustain the cash-flow position from other fund income, are making an informed decision. The members who do not do this arithmetic are making a guess.

The SMSF as a Family Structure: Multi-Generational Considerations

One of the lesser-discussed features of the SMSF structure is its capacity to function as a multi-generational family financial structure. Under the 2021 amendments that increased the maximum membership from four to six, an SMSF can now include members spanning 2 generations of a family — parents and adult children, for example — within a single legal structure.

The advantages of a multi-generational SMSF structure are significant. Investment costs are shared across a larger total balance, improving the fee efficiency for all members. Estate planning can be coordinated across the family unit, with investment strategy and death benefit nominations designed to work in concert. And where the family includes business owners with commercial property, the business real property rules can facilitate property ownership arrangements that benefit multiple family members.

The disadvantages are equally significant and deserve careful consideration. All members are co-trustees and carry equal legal responsibility for the fund's compliance. If 1 member makes a decision that produces a compliance breach, all members are potentially liable. The social dynamics of family co-trustees — parents and adult children managing financial decisions together, potentially with different risk tolerances, different investment preferences, and different retirement timelines — can be challenging. And the death or incapacity of any member creates administration complexity that affects all members.

My general recommendation for multi-generational SMSF structures: they are appropriate where the family members have strong communication, aligned financial values, and a genuine shared benefit from the combined structure. They are inappropriate where family dynamics are complicated, where members have fundamentally different investment philosophies, or where the primary motivation is simply fee splitting rather than genuine shared planning. The legal obligation of trusteeship does not respect family relationships — every co-trustee is equally responsible, regardless of whether they feel included in the decision-making process.

Multi-Gen SMSF: Pros	Multi-Gen SMSF: Cons
Shared administration costs across larger balance	Shared legal liability for all trustee decisions
Coordinated estate planning across generations	Potential for conflicting investment preferences

Business real property benefits for family business	Complex trustee succession when older generation dies
Tax efficiency through pension phase timing	Social dynamics complicate financial decision-making
6-member maximum provides flexibility	Every member must be trustee (or director of corporate trustee)

The Sole Member SMSF: A Special Case

A single-member SMSF — where the fund has only 1 member — is a permissible but structurally distinct arrangement. The SIS Act requires that a single-member SMSF either have a corporate trustee (with the member as sole director), or have two individual trustees (the member and one other person who is not an employer of the member, unless the employer is a related company).

The sole member SMSF is common among self-employed professionals and business owners who have not yet partnered with a spouse or whose spouse's superannuation is managed separately. The advantages are clear: complete control over investment decisions, complete clarity about whose interests the fund is serving, and no trustee coordination issues. The disadvantages are equally clear: the lack of a co-trustee means there is no second pair of eyes on investment or compliance decisions, the death or incapacity of the sole member creates an immediate governance crisis, and the corporate trustee structure (strongly recommended) adds ongoing administrative cost.

For sole member SMSFs, the corporate trustee is not just strongly recommended — it is, in my view, essential. A sole member who is also the sole individual trustee of their SMSF has a structural governance problem: there is literally no one else in the decision-making chain. A corporate trustee, with the member as sole director and a nominated successor director in the event of death or incapacity, provides the minimum governance structure that a sole member SMSF requires to function safely across the full potential life of the fund.

Chapter Three
The Weight of Trusteeship

You asked for control. Here is what comes with it.

There is a moment that many new SMSF trustees experience, usually somewhere between 3 and 12 months after establishing their fund. It arrives when they are reviewing the trustee responsibilities documentation their adviser has prepared, or when they are signing the annual compliance declaration, or when they first sit down with their auditor. The moment is a kind of vertigo — a sudden, disorienting recognition of the full weight of what they have taken on.

David, who established his SMSF in early 2023, described it precisely: 'I thought establishing an SMSF meant investment freedom. I never realised how many responsibilities came with it. When I sat down with a 50-page trustee checklist 3 months in, I actually felt cold. One mistake in the wrong area, and everything I had built could be gone.'

The vertigo is appropriate. Being an SMSF trustee is not a formality. It is a legal status that carries specific, enforceable obligations — obligations that extend well beyond the investment decisions and compliance forms that most people associate with running a superannuation fund. These obligations can be enforced by the ATO, by other fund members, and by courts. The penalties for breaching them can include substantial fines, disqualification from acting as a trustee, and personal liability for any losses the fund suffers as a result of the breach.

This chapter examines what those obligations actually are. We begin with a court case that illustrates, with uncomfortable precision, what happens when a trustee allows personal interests to override professional duties.

The $250,000 Lesson: When Business Partners Become Adversaries

In 1995, David Henderson and Robert Connelly had been business partners for 9 years. They had built a successful import business together, shared an office, and trusted each other completely. When David suggested they establish a joint SMSF, Robert agreed immediately. They each contributed $300,000, becoming co-trustees and co-members of what would, for the next 5 years, be an unremarkable but successful small superannuation fund.

By 2000, things had changed. A dispute over the direction of their business had created a rift. Lawyers were involved. The professional relationship — and the personal one — was deteriorating. David decided he wanted to exit the SMSF and transfer his entitlement, which had grown to $420,000, to a new fund.

Robert refused to sign the transfer documents.

His stated reasons shifted over the following months. First, he argued that the underlying commercial dispute needed to be resolved before fund matters could be addressed. Then he raised concerns about the interest calculation methodology. Then he claimed the fund's investment strategy needed review before any capital could be withdrawn. None of these objections had any legal foundation, but each one provided another month's delay.

Over 18 months, David's $420,000 sat frozen in the joint SMSF while the broader market rose 15%. The money could not be reinvested in David's preferred strategy. It could not be transferred to capture the market gains. It was effectively held hostage by his co-trustee's refusal to cooperate.

David's opportunity cost: $63,000 — the return he would have earned if the transfer had proceeded on schedule.

He sued.

The Court's Findings: Three Simultaneous Violations

The Supreme Court of Victoria's judgment in this matter (based on the principles established in Dunstone v Irving [2000] VSC) was unambiguous and, for Robert, devastating.

The court found that Robert had simultaneously breached three distinct legal obligations:

First, he had violated the fund's trust deed, which required trustees to cooperate with members' lawful entitlement transfers. The right to transfer his accumulated benefits was David's legal entitlement under the trust deed. Robert's refusal was not a legitimate exercise of trustee discretion — it was a direct violation of the document he had signed when the fund was established.

Second, he had violated the statutory SIS deed — the obligations implied into every SMSF trust deed by the SIS Act, regardless of what the trust deed itself says. Among these obligations is the requirement that trustees act in the interests of the fund's members. Robert was acting in his own interests — specifically, his interest in using the fund as a bargaining chip in the commercial dispute — not in David's interests as a fund member.

Third, he had violated the common law duties of a trustee — principles developed over centuries of equity jurisprudence that require trustees to act in good faith, without conflict of interest, and in accordance with the trust's purpose. Commercial disputes between business partners are not a legitimate basis for refusing to comply with a member's lawful entitlement.

> **$250,000 Robert's personal liability — Dunstone v Irving [2000]**
>
> Compensation components: opportunity cost loss $63,000 + legal costs $120,000 + interest and punitive damages $67,000. Payable personally by Robert — not from the SMSF's assets. This is the most important aspect of the judgment: trustee breach liability is personal. The SMSF cannot absorb it.

The $250,000 judgment against Robert was not paid by the SMSF. It was paid by Robert personally, from his own assets. This is one of the most important aspects of SMSF trustee liability that people consistently underestimate: when you breach your duties as a trustee, you are personally liable for the consequences. The fund's assets are not available to absorb your mistakes.

> **Robert's Reflection**
>
> *"I thought I was protecting the fund. The court found I was destroying it.*
>
> *"I mixed up the commercial dispute with the fund. They are completely separate legal matters. The ATO — and courts — do not accept personal grievances as a basis for failing to perform trustee duties.*
>
> *"I thought refusing to sign was just leverage. I never understood that refusing to process a member's legitimate entitlement was a serious legal breach.*
>
> *"The $250,000 I paid personally taught me something that should have been obvious: a trustee role is not a position — it is a legal obligation."*

The Three-Layer Duty System

Robert's case is a useful introduction to SMSF trustee obligations because it illustrates a principle that many trustees do not fully appreciate: the obligations do not come from a single source. They stack. They overlap. And they all apply simultaneously.

Understanding the three-layer structure of trustee duties is essential to understanding why compliance failures are often more serious than trustees expect, and why seemingly 'minor' breaches can have major consequences.

Layer One: Common Law Trustee Duties

These are the duties that courts have developed over centuries of equity jurisprudence. They pre-date the SIS Act by hundreds of years and apply to all trustees, not just those managing superannuation funds. They include the duty to act in the interests of beneficiaries, the duty of loyalty (to avoid conflicts of interest), the duty of care (to exercise the level of care and skill that a prudent person would exercise), and the duty to act unanimously when there is more than 1 trustee.

Common law duties are not codified — they exist in case precedent, accumulated across thousands of decisions. This makes them both broad and somewhat unpredictable. Courts have significant latitude in applying them to specific circumstances. The consequence is that common law duties can catch trustees who believe they have complied with the SIS Act and their trust deed but have nonetheless acted in a way that a court characterises as a breach of their fundamental obligations.

Layer Two: The Statutory SIS Deed

The SIS Act implies certain covenants into every SMSF trust deed — regardless of whether those covenants appear explicitly in the trust deed itself. These are the minimum standards that all SMSF trustees must meet as a matter of law.

The core SIS deed covenants include: the duty to formulate and give effect to an investment strategy that takes into account the fund's circumstances; the duty to act honestly in all matters; the duty not to use the fund's assets for personal purposes; and the duty to consider the appropriateness of each investment in the context of the fund's overall portfolio.

The SIS Act also imposes specific prohibitions — on lending to members, on acquiring assets from related parties, on allowing members to benefit currently from the fund — that are the subject of Chapter Four.

Layer Three: The Trust Deed

The fund's own trust deed — the document that establishes the specific rules governing this particular SMSF — is the third layer. It can impose requirements over and above the common law and SIS Act obligations, but it cannot override them. In practice, most professionally drafted trust deeds closely mirror the SIS Act requirements, but they often contain additional provisions about investment decision-making, member entitlements, and trustee indemnification.

Violating the trust deed is a legal breach, even if the conduct also violated the SIS Act and common law. All 3 sources of obligation are live simultaneously. A trustee who believes they have satisfied the SIS Act but neglected the trust deed is still in breach.

Layer	Source	Character	Typical Enforcement
Common Law	Centuries of case precedent	Broad, interpretive, equity-based	Court action by aggrieved members
SIS Act (s52B)	Federal legislation	Specific, prescriptive, detailed	ATO penalties and prosecutions
Trust Deed	Fund's founding document	Specific to this fund	Court action or ATO review
All Three	Simultaneously applicable	Cannot be individually waived	Multiple simultaneous exposures

The Sole Purpose Test: SMSF's Foundational Rule

Of all the obligations that flow through the three-layer duty system, none is more fundamental — or more frequently misunderstood — than the Sole Purpose Test.

Section 62 of the SIS Act requires that an SMSF trustee maintain the fund 'solely' for one or more of three core purposes: providing benefits to members at or after retirement; providing benefits to members at or after age 65; or providing death benefits to members' dependants.

The critical word is 'solely.' Not 'primarily.' Not 'mainly.' Solely.

This is not a semantic distinction. It is the difference between compliance and catastrophic non-compliance.

A fund that is maintained 99% for retirement savings and 1% for any other purpose — even a benevolent, family-oriented, seemingly harmless purpose — fails the Sole Purpose Test. The consequences of that failure include the fund being declared non-complying and all of its assets being taxed at 45%.

Jennifer's $191,250 Lesson: The Cost of a $250-a-Week Kindness

Jennifer Chen was 52 years old, a Sydney accountant who had built her SMSF over 10 years to a balance of $800,000. She was meticulous about compliance — her investment strategy was current, her audits were on time, her financial statements were impeccable.

In 2020, her daughter Lisa graduated from university and took a position at a technology company in Chatswood. Sydney's rental market was brutal, and Lisa was struggling to find affordable accommodation near her office.

Jennifer had a solution. Her SMSF held $300,000 in cash that she had been intending to invest in property. She decided to bring forward that investment: she would purchase a two-bedroom apartment in Chatswood, near Lisa's office, and rent it to her daughter.

The market rent for comparable properties in the area was $650 per week. Jennifer offered Lisa a 'family rate' of $400 per week, reasoning that it was still meaningful rent — not free housing — but affordable for a recent graduate. The SMSF would still receive rental income. Lisa would save $250 a week compared to the market. Everyone would benefit.

'It's my fund,' Jennifer reasoned. 'I make the decisions. I'm not giving her the property — I'm just being fair with the rent.'

Her accountant raised an objection in the clearest possible terms. Jennifer overrode it.

The ATO's Analysis

In 2023, during a routine data-matching review, the ATO identified the below-market rental arrangement. The audit notice arrived 3 months later.

The ATO's finding was straightforward. The fund had purchased a property at market rates and then rented it to a related party — the member's daughter — at a price 36% below market. The ATO's view: the purpose of this investment was not solely to provide Jennifer with retirement benefits. At least part of its purpose was to provide Jennifer's daughter with affordable housing. That purpose — however kind, however familial, however modest in scale — was a 'current benefit' that failed the Sole Purpose Test.

The ATO's determination: the fund was non-complying for the 3 years from 2020 to 2022.

Category	Amount	Calculation
Rental income (3 years)	$62,400	$20,800 × 3 years

Property appreciation	$80,000	$300K → $380K
Share portfolio appreciation	$100,000	$500K → $600K
Total taxable income	$242,400	All fund income taxed at 45%
Tax at 45%	$109,080	$242,400 × 45%
ATO penalty	$30,000	Sole Purpose Test breach
Legal and professional fees	$35,000	Adviser + lawyer response
Interest and charges	$17,170	Late payment
TOTAL COST	$191,250	Cost of saving Jennifer's daughter $250/week

The cost-benefit analysis is almost too painful to contemplate. The rent savings Jennifer provided to her daughter over 3 years: $250 per week × 52 weeks × 3 years = $39,000. The cost to Jennifer's SMSF: $191,250. The ratio: for every $1 Jennifer's daughter saved, Jennifer's fund lost $4.90.

The accountant, on receiving the ATO's determination, called Jennifer immediately. There was nothing to say that she had not already warned her about. She said it anyway: 'Jennifer, I told you exactly what would happen. You should have listened.'

Jennifer knew. That was the worst part. She had listened to her family instincts and overridden her professional judgment. The cost was $191,250 and an ATO monitoring flag that would follow her fund for 5 years.

$191,250 Jennifer's total cost for a $39,000 act of generosity

3 years of $250/week rent savings for her daughter: $39,000 benefit. SMSF cost: $191,250. Net family loss: $152,250. The correct approach would have been to gift her daughter $39,000 in cash — legal, tax-efficient, and $152,250 cheaper.

What the Sole Purpose Test Actually Prohibits

Jennifer's case establishes several important principles, but it is far from the only form in which Sole Purpose Test violations occur. The following categories cover the most common breaches:

Direct Use — The Member Enjoys the Asset

The most obvious violation is when the member uses a fund asset for personal purposes. Holiday properties used occasionally by the family. Motor vehicles driven on weekends. Artwork displayed in the member's home. Wine stored in the member's cellar. Boats used for weekend recreational sailing. Any personal use of a fund-owned asset, regardless of frequency or proportion, violates the Sole Purpose Test.

The ATO's position on frequency and proportion is unambiguous: even 1% personal use is non-compliant. Even 1 day a year. Even one drive in the vintage car. The test is 'solely' — and solely is absolute.

Related Party Benefit — Someone Else Enjoys an Advantage

The violation does not require personal use by the member. If the fund's investment decision is shaped — even partially — by the desire to benefit a related party, the Sole Purpose Test is breached. Jennifer's case is the archetypal example: she was not going to live in the apartment herself, but the investment decision was structured to benefit her daughter.

Leasing commercial property to a member's business at below-market rates. Investing in a company where the member's spouse is an employee on above-market salary. Allowing a family member to store personal belongings in a fund-owned warehouse. Financing a related party's business venture on terms more favourable than a commercial lender would provide. All of these arrangements create 'current benefits' — advantages enjoyed now, before retirement — that violate the test.

Current Benefit to the Member

Even where no related party benefits, the member can violate the Sole Purpose Test by obtaining current personal advantage from the fund. The most common examples are loans from the fund (discussed in Chapter Four), guarantees provided by the fund for the member's personal borrowings, or the fund effectively serving as a vehicle for the member's business activities rather than pure retirement savings.

The Aussiegolfa Case: Where the Line Actually Is

Given Jennifer's outcome, a natural question arises: can an SMSF ever rent to related parties at all? The answer — provided by a landmark 2018 Full Federal Court decision — is yes, under very specific circumstances.

The case involved the Benson Family Super Fund. The fund's trustee company, Aussiegolfa Pty Ltd, had purchased a residential investment property in 2011 through a managed investment scheme. For the first 2 years, the property was rented to two unrelated tenants at the prevailing market rate of $500 per week. In 2013, the member's daughter became the tenant — also at $500 per week.

The ATO argued that renting to a related party, even at market rates, violated the Sole Purpose Test because it provided the daughter with a 'current benefit' — stable accommodation near a family property.

The Full Federal Court disagreed. On the specific facts of this case, it found no breach. The key findings:

- The rent was at market rates — identical to what previous unrelated tenants had paid.
- There was no evidence that the fund's investment strategy had been modified because of the daughter's tenancy.
- The property had been rented to unrelated parties for 2 years before the daughter became a tenant — suggesting the investment decision was made independently of the desire to house the daughter.
- There was no evidence that the fund was being maintained with any purpose other than retirement savings.

The court was careful to note what it was not deciding. It was not creating a rule that 'market rate = compliant.' Rather, it was finding that on these specific facts — with the specific sequencing, the specific evidence of investment independence, the specific absence of any strategy modification — there was no breach.

The ATO's response to the judgment was equally careful. The ATO explicitly stated that it did not accept the case as authority for a general proposition that related-party tenancies at market rates are permissible. The decisive question, the ATO confirmed, is the purpose for which the investment was made. If the purpose included providing accommodation to a related party — even at market rates — a breach could still be found.

Factor	Jennifer (Breach)	Aussiegolfa (No Breach)
Rental rate	$400/week (36% below market)	$500/week (100% market rate)
Investment timing	Purchased for daughter's use	Purchased 2 years before daughter moved in
Strategy modification?	Strategy adjusted to accommodate daughter	No evidence of strategy impact

Evidence of purpose	Explicitly to provide affordable housing	No evidence of incidental purpose
Outcome	Non-complying fund, $191,250 total cost	Compliant

The practical rule for trustees: if you are considering renting a fund asset to a related party, the answer should almost always be 'no' unless you have very clear written professional advice that your specific arrangement satisfies the requirements. The risk of getting this wrong is enormous. The ATO has wide discretionary powers in this area, the courts have shown that very fine factual distinctions can be determinative, and the cost of non-compliance is catastrophic.

The Trustee's Practical Obligations: A Complete Picture

Beyond the Sole Purpose Test, SMSF trustees carry a range of specific obligations that are imposed by the SIS Act and must be satisfied every year, without exception.

The Investment Strategy Requirement

Section 52B of the SIS Act requires that SMSF trustees formulate, regularly review, and give effect to an investment strategy. This is not a filing formality — it is a substantive obligation.

A valid SMSF investment strategy must consider: the risk profile of the investments relative to the fund's objectives; the likely return of the investments relative to the objectives; the liquidity of the investments relative to the fund's expected cash flow requirements (including pension payments); the ability to meet any liability the fund may have; and the level of diversification across the portfolio.

'Formulate' means the strategy must exist in writing, be specific, and be signed by the trustees. 'Regularly review' means it must be assessed at least annually and updated whenever the fund's circumstances or investment mix changes materially. 'Give effect to' means the fund's actual investments must be consistent with the strategy — you cannot have a strategy that specifies diversified investments while the fund holds 90% in a single asset class.

Lisa's $85,000 loss in Chapter Four is partly attributable to making a substantial investment without first updating the investment strategy. Mark's $420,000 loss demonstrates how the in-house asset rule under s 71 activates the moment a related party steps into the picture — and how that moment, combined with NALI consequences and liquidity problems, can compound dramatically.

The Annual Audit Requirement

Every SMSF must be audited annually by an approved SMSF auditor — a person registered with ASIC and licensed to provide SMSF audit services. The auditor must be independent of the fund: they cannot be a member, a trustee, the fund's accountant, or in any other related-party relationship with the fund.

The audit has 2 components: the financial audit (examining whether the fund's financial statements fairly represent its position and performance) and the compliance audit (examining whether the fund has satisfied the SIS Act's requirements during the year). The auditor reports any breaches to the ATO.

A fund whose audit is not completed on time is in breach. A fund that fails to provide its auditor with complete and accurate records is in breach. A fund whose auditor identifies compliance issues and the trustees do not address them is in breach. The audit is the primary mechanism through which compliance problems are identified — which means that a well-run fund with a rigorous auditor is actually the safest possible structure, because problems are caught early. Michael's fund, with its inadequate record-keeping and its delayed audits, had no equivalent safety net.

The Trustee Declaration

Every person who becomes a new SMSF trustee or director of a corporate trustee must sign a trustee declaration form (NAT 71089) within 21 days of their appointment. This declaration acknowledges that the signatory understands their obligations and has read the relevant ATO guidance.

This is not merely an administrative form. Courts have treated the trustee declaration as evidence that a trustee understood their obligations. A trustee who signs the declaration and then breaches the obligations they have declared understanding of is in a significantly worse position than a trustee who never had the opportunity to be informed.

Personal Liability: The Most Sobering Aspect of Trusteeship

Throughout this chapter, we have seen examples of trustee liability. Robert's $250,000 judgment was payable from his personal assets. Jennifer's $191,250 in penalties and professional costs was borne by her fund, but the compliance monitoring and reputational consequences were hers alone. In Chapter Four, we will see trustees who face simultaneous administrative penalties, disqualification orders, and civil liability.

The most important principle to understand is this: being an SMSF trustee creates personal liability that the fund's assets cannot absorb. When you breach your trustee obligations, the consequences fall on you — not the fund.

This includes administrative penalties. Under the SIS Act, administrative penalties are assessed against the trustee personally, not the fund. When the ATO imposes a $19,800 penalty for a Sole Purpose Test breach, that amount is owed by you, as an individual. Your SMSF's assets cannot pay it. (Some corporate trustee structures provide some mitigation, which is 1 reason corporate trustees are recommended, but the liability itself remains personal in most cases.)

This includes compensation to harmed members. If a trustee's breach causes another fund member to suffer a loss, the breaching trustee is liable to compensate that member personally. Robert's $420,000 opportunity cost was the central element in the $250,000 judgment against him.

This also includes criminal liability in extreme cases. Intentional misuse of SMSF assets, deliberate fraud, and repeated serious non-compliance can result in criminal prosecution under the SIS Act's penalty provisions, including custodial sentences.

The Reality Check: What Trustee Liability Actually Means

When your SMSF adviser talks about 'trustee liability,' this is what they mean:

Administrative penalties: $6,600 to $19,800 per breach, payable personally.

Civil liability: Compensation to other fund members for losses caused by your breach.

Fund penalties: The fund's non-complying status taxing all assets at 45%.

Disqualification: Inability to act as a trustee for up to 5 years (or permanently for serious breaches).

Criminal liability: In extreme cases, custodial sentences for intentional misuse or fraud.

Every time you sign a trustee document, make an investment decision, or approve a transaction, you are exercising this legal power — and accepting this personal liability. This is why 'professional support' is not a luxury item in SMSF management. It is the infrastructure that prevents these outcomes.

Practical Guidance: How to Run a Compliant SMSF

After reading this chapter, you might feel that the weight of trustee responsibility is almost impossibly heavy. In practice, it is not — provided you have the right infrastructure and the right habits. The following guidance is drawn from 10 years of advising compliant, well-run SMSFs.

Essential Infrastructure

- Engage a qualified SMSF specialist adviser for investment strategy and lifecycle decisions.
- Appoint an experienced SMSF accountant for annual financial statements and tax compliance.
- Use an independent licensed SMSF auditor who will review both financial and compliance aspects rigorously.
- Establish a corporate trustee structure — it simplifies member changes and provides cleaner legal separation.
- Use a professionally prepared trust deed drafted by a firm specialising in SMSF law, not a generic online document.

Annual Habits

- Review and update the investment strategy before the end of each financial year — even if nothing has changed, the review itself should be documented.
- Provide the auditor with complete, well-organised records for every transaction during the year.
- Review the auditor's report carefully and address any issues raised within the deadline the auditor specifies.
- Attend at least one formal trustee meeting per year with your co-trustees, document the decisions made, and keep the minutes.
- Before making any investment decision, ask 3 questions: Does this satisfy the Sole Purpose Test? Does it comply with

the investment strategy? Does it violate any SIS Act prohibition?

The One Question That Saves Thousands

Every experienced SMSF adviser has a version of this test, and I have found no better formulation than this one:

> **The Trustee's Core Question**
>
> Before every investment decision, ask yourself: 'If this related party relationship, or this family connection, or this personal desire did not exist, would I make exactly the same investment decision for exactly the same investment reasons?'
>
> If the answer is 'yes' — if the investment would be equally attractive to you as a purely commercial proposition, regardless of who benefits from it or uses it — then you are likely in safe territory.
>
> If the answer is 'no' — if the related party connection is part of why the investment makes sense — then you are walking toward a Sole Purpose Test violation, and the cost of proceeding is almost certainly much higher than whatever benefit you believe the arrangement provides.

Chapter Three Summary

Being an SMSF trustee is one of the most powerful financial roles available to an Australian individual. It confers genuine, substantive control over a substantial and growing pool of retirement assets. But that power comes with genuine, substantive legal obligations — obligations imposed simultaneously by centuries of equity jurisprudence, federal superannuation legislation, and the fund's own founding document.

The cases in this chapter — Robert's $250,000 personal judgment and Jennifer's $191,250 penalty — are not edge cases or cautionary tales about exceptional recklessness. They are examples of exactly the kind of error that intelligent, careful people make when they do not fully understand the rules they are operating under. Robert was a successful businessman who thought he was protecting the fund. Jennifer was a professional accountant who knew the rules but chose to override them for family reasons.

Both paid a severe price.

Obligation	Source	Key Requirement	Cost of Breach
Act in members' interests	Common law + SIS s52B	Always, even in disputes with other members	Personal liability for losses
Investment strategy	SIS s52B	Written, reviewed annually, actually followed	$6,600-$19,800 penalty per breach
Sole Purpose Test	SIS s62	Solely for retirement — no current benefits	Non-complying: 45% tax on all assets
Annual audit	SIS s35C	Independent, licensed auditor, on time	Penalties + ATO scrutiny
Trustee declaration	SIS s104A	Signed within 21 days of appointment	Personal liability; evidence of knowledge
Record keeping	SIS s103	5-10 years depending on document type	Audit qualification; ATO penalties

In Chapter Four, we move to the investment rules that govern what an SMSF can and cannot invest in. These rules are specific, absolute, and — as 8 case studies will demonstrate — extraordinarily expensive to violate.

The 5 Sources of Trustee Failure: A Pattern Analysis

In ten years of practice, I have seen SMSF trustees fail in a reasonably predictable set of ways. The failures are not random. They cluster around specific points in the fund's lifecycle and specific characteristics of the trustees involved. Understanding these patterns is not an exercise in pessimism — it is the foundation of prevention.

Failure Pattern	Typical Trigger	Frequency in My Practice
Delegation without oversight	Trusted administrator or accountant makes errors without review	Most common — approximately 35% of cases
Related party transaction creep	Gradual normalisation of small related party benefits	Second most common — approximately 25% of cases
Lifecycle blindness	Rules that applied at 55 do not apply at 68; failure to track age-based changes	Approximately 20% of cases
Estate planning neglect	Deferred BDBN, lapsed nomination, misaligned will	Approximately 12% of cases

Complexity overreach	LRBA, property, and illiquid assets without supporting cash flow	Approximately 8% of cases

Delegation without oversight deserves particular emphasis, because it is the most common failure pattern and the one that trustees are least likely to self-identify. The scenario is consistent: a trustee engages a competent-seeming professional to manage the SMSF's compliance. They receive annual reports that appear complete. The audit is clean. They sign what they are given and file it. And then, five or seven or 10 years later, an audit or a new adviser discovers that a series of small errors have accumulated into a significant compliance problem — excess contributions that were never flagged, valuations that were not updated, a related party transaction that was improperly documented.

The trustee in these cases is not malicious. They are trusting — which is an admirable quality that the compliance environment of an SMSF punishes when it is not paired with engagement. The trustee obligation is not satisfied by signing documents. It is satisfied by understanding what you are signing, why it matters, and what a different answer would look like.

How Professional Oversight Works in Practice

The trustees who navigate the compliance environment most successfully are not the ones with the deepest technical knowledge. They are the ones with the most productive professional relationships — where they know enough to ask the right questions, where they engage proactively rather than reactively, and where they have established a rhythm of annual review that prevents the accumulation of small problems into large ones.

Specifically, what that looks like in practice: an annual review meeting with your financial adviser and accountant, ideally in April or May before the financial year ends, that covers contributions planning, investment strategy review, compliance status, and a forward-looking assessment of any upcoming lifecycle changes. A separate, periodic review — every two to 3 years — of the structural elements: trust deed currency, BDBN validity, insurance adequacy, and death benefit planning alignment with the current will.

The cost of this level of engagement is modest: perhaps two to 3 hours of adviser time per year beyond the standard compliance work, at professional rates. The benefit is the systematic prevention of the compound-interest effect of small, deferred compliance problems.

The Audit Relationship: Your Last Line of Defence

Every SMSF must have its financial accounts and compliance obligations audited annually by an ASIC-registered, approved SMSF auditor. The auditor must be independent — they cannot audit a fund in which they have any financial interest, and they cannot audit a fund managed by a firm of which they are a partner.

The audit is not a rubber-stamp process, although some trustees treat it as one. A competent SMSF auditor will review the fund's financial accounts for accuracy, examine investment valuations for reasonableness, check that contributions fall within caps, verify that pension payments meet minimum requirements, and review the fund's compliance with the SIS Act's investment restrictions. The audit produces a report that the trustees and the ATO can both see.

When an auditor identifies a compliance breach, they are required by law to report it to the ATO. This is called a contravention report, and it is the mechanism by which the ATO becomes aware of compliance issues that the trustees may not have self-reported. Trustees who discover a compliance issue and seek to remediate it proactively — before the audit — are in a significantly better position than those whose breaches are identified at audit. Voluntary disclosure to the ATO, under its SMSF Voluntary Disclosure Service, can substantially reduce penalties for trustees who come forward before an audit or ATO review identifies the issue.

> **If You Discover a Compliance Breach — Act Immediately**
>
> Do not wait for the annual audit. Contact your SMSF adviser or accountant the moment you identify or suspect a compliance issue. Early engagement gives you access to the ATO's Voluntary Disclosure Service, which can substantially reduce penalties. Silence does not make compliance issues disappear — it makes them compound.

Related Party Transactions: The Grey Zone Between Legal and Illegal

The related party transaction rules are among the most frequently misunderstood in SMSF law. Most trustees understand the broad prohibition: the fund generally cannot deal with related parties on favourable terms. What many do not understand is where the boundary of 'related party' lies, what 'favourable terms' means in practice, and what the specific exceptions to the prohibition are.

Who Is a Related Party?

The SIS Act defines a related party as: any member of the fund; a standard employer-sponsor of the fund; and various 'associates' of members and employer-sponsors. The definition of associate is broad. It includes relatives (spouse, children, parents, grandparents, brothers, sisters, and their respective spouses and children), business partners, and any company or trust in which the member or their associate has a controlling interest (typically 50% or more).

The practical implications: if you own 51% of a company, that company is your associate and therefore a related party of your SMSF. Your SMSF cannot lend money to that company. It cannot buy assets from that company at below-market rates. It cannot rent commercial property to that company at below-market rates. The same restrictions apply to your spouse's business interests, your children's business interests, and any trust in which you are a beneficiary with a controlling interest.

Related Party Category	Examples	SMSF Restrictions
Direct member	The trustee themselves	Cannot borrow from fund; cannot receive current day-to-day benefits
Spouse of member	De facto partners included	Same restrictions as member; all assets jointly owned subject to rules
Children (any age)	Adult and minor children	Cannot be a borrower from the fund; property cannot be used personally
Company controlled by member	Director or 50%+ shareholder	Cannot borrow; cannot transact on non-arm's length terms; NALI risk
Trust controlled by member	Family discretionary trust with member as trustee/appointor	Same as company — arm's length requirements apply to all transactions
Business partner	Partner in professional firm	Associate status applies to partnership business dealings with SMSF

The 'Arm's Length' Test in Practice

Where a transaction between an SMSF and a related party is permitted — for example, renting business real property to a related party's business — it must be conducted on arm's length terms. This means the price, rent, or rate must be the same as what an independent third party would pay in the open market. It is not sufficient that the parties believe the terms are fair. The terms must be evidenced by market comparisons.

For rental of commercial property, this means an independent property valuation and rental appraisal from a licensed valuer or real estate agent, conducted at the commencement of the tenancy and reviewed at regular intervals (typically annually or on each renewal). The rent paid must match the market rent. If the market rate changes — if comparable commercial properties in the area are renting for more — the rent must be reviewed and adjusted upward accordingly. Charging a related party below-market rent, even from a position of genuine generosity or family loyalty, is a Non-Arm's Length Income (NALI) trigger.

I have had trustees tell me that they know the market rate is higher but have not increased the rent because 'the business is struggling.' I understand the impulse. It is financially generous, personally kind, and professionally catastrophic. The ATO does not distinguish between below-market rent caused by ignorance and below-market rent caused by deliberately supporting a struggling family business. The tax consequence is identical: non-arm's length income, assessed at 45%, permanently on that asset.

Jennifer's Update: 4 Years Later

When I last had contact with Jennifer Chen — whose $191,250 NALI case anchors the main text of Chapter Three — she had resolved the immediate compliance issue by selling the Chatswood apartment (outside superannuation) and replacing it with a commercial strata property that her SMSF acquired from an unrelated vendor on the open market. Her daughter Lisa continued to use the property, at market rent, as her physiotherapy practice. The commercial property was performing well. The transition had cost Jennifer approximately $45,000 in stamp duty, legal fees, and agent commissions — but had eliminated the permanent NALI contamination that would have accumulated for decades on the original residential property.

Jennifer's reflection on the experience: 'I thought I was being smart. I thought I was finding a way to help my daughter while also building my own retirement. Nobody explained to me that in superannuation law, that combination is exactly what triggers the NALI rules. I wish I had known years earlier. The transition was expensive, but it was far less expensive than continuing down the road I was on.'

I include her reflection not as a lesson in regret but as an example of something I see consistently in clients who have navigated compliance failures: the moment of clear-eyed acknowledgment that the cost of the solution is far less than the cost of continuation. The trustees who do best are not those who never make errors — it is impossible to manage a complex regulatory structure for 10 years without error. They are the ones who find their errors quickly, acknowledge them honestly, and fix them efficiently.

Chapter Four
The Investment Red Lines

Six absolute rules. 8 case studies. $1,974,000 in preventable losses.

There is a question I am sometimes asked at seminars that reveals a fundamental misunderstanding about SMSF investment law: 'Can I invest in anything I want, as long as it makes money?'

The answer is no. And the cost of discovering that answer through experience rather than education is, on average, $246,750 per case.

The SIS Act imposes a comprehensive set of investment restrictions on SMSFs. These restrictions are not guidelines or best practices — they are absolute legal prohibitions. They apply regardless of whether the investment is profitable. They apply regardless of whether other parties consented. They apply regardless of how carefully the transaction was structured to appear compliant. Courts and the ATO have consistently and repeatedly held that these rules mean exactly what they say.

In this chapter, we examine six of the most important of these restrictions through 8 case studies that collectively cost their subjects nearly two million dollars. We begin with a prologue that shows, in a single comparative tableau, the full range of outcomes that flow from the same starting position.

Prologue: Three SMSFs, Three Destinies

In early 2024, three professionals — all 50 years old, all with $1,000,000 in their SMSFs — made their investment decisions. 3 years later, in 2027, their funds had arrived at outcomes separated by more than a million dollars.

Robert: The Man Who Thought He Made the Rules

Robert was a property developer. He had been making investment decisions for 30 years, and most of them had been good ones. He was confident, decisive, and not inclined to seek permission for decisions he had already made.

His SMSF investment plan for 2024:

$700,000 to purchase development land from his own property development company. The land had an independent market value of approximately $500,000, but Robert reasoned that the premium he was paying to his company was 'fair' because his company had carried development risk on the site. He set the transfer price at $700,000.

$200,000 as a working capital loan to his company. Interest rate: 2% per year, compared to the commercial rate of 6%.

$100,000 in cash.

The rationalisations were seamless. He knew the company better than any external buyer. The arrangement was 'mutually beneficial.' The premium was 'commercially justified.' The low interest rate was offset by the security he had over the loan.

In July 2025, the ATO's compliance review arrived.

The determination was efficient and brutal. Section 66 of the SIS Act prohibits an SMSF from acquiring assets from related parties, except in three narrow categories. Development land held by a related-party company is not in any of those categories. Section 65 prohibits lending to members or related parties, with no exceptions whatsoever. The $700,000 purchase was illegal. The $200,000 loan was illegal. The $200,000 overvalue above market price constituted a non-arm's length transaction.

Consequences: fund deemed non-complying for 2024-25; all income taxed at 45%; administrative penalties of $42,840; immediate disposal order for non-compliant assets within 90 days.

The disposal was devastating. The development land — purchased for $700,000 — was sold under time pressure for $450,000. Loss: $250,000. The loan — $200,000 advanced at 2% — was structured as an illegal contract and legally unenforceable. The company could not recover. Loss: $200,000.

> **$700,000 → $300,000 Robert's SMSF: 70% reduction in 3 years**
>
> Starting balance: $1,000,000. Development land loss: $250,000 (forced sale at $450K vs $700K purchase). Company loan loss: $200,000 (illegal contract, irrecoverable). Tax penalties: $19,500. Administrative penalties: $42,840. Total losses: ~$700,000. Robert's comment: 'I thought I had control over everything. I didn't understand how serious the rules are.'

Sarah: The Investor Who Understood That Rules Are Protection

Sarah took a different approach. She engaged a specialist SMSF adviser before making any investment decision. The adviser reviewed her investment strategy, modelled several scenarios, and recommended a portfolio that was structured around compliance from the beginning.

Her $1,000,000 allocation: $400,000 in a Vanguard ASX 200 ETF; $300,000 in a commercial property in Parramatta, financed through an LRBA with a $200,000 Westpac loan, leased to an unrelated third-party accounting firm at market rent of $45,000 annually; $200,000 in Australian government bonds; $100,000 in a high-interest savings account.

Her investment strategy was a specific, detailed document: asset allocation ranges, liquidity requirements, risk parameters, and a compliance statement confirming compliance with the SIS Act's investment prohibitions. Annual review scheduled for January.

3 years later, Sarah's SMSF had grown to $1,385,000 — a 38% return. Not a single compliance issue. Not a single penalty. The commercial property had appreciated to $380,000. The ETF had returned 8.5% per year. The annual audit was a formality.

Sarah's observation: 'I paid $3,000 to a professional to design my investment strategy. That was the best investment I made. 3 years of 38% growth with zero compliance issues. I sleep very well.'

> **$1,000,000 → $1,385,000**
> **Sarah's SMSF: 38% growth in 3 years**
>
> Fully compliant structure. Commenced pension transition at 53. On track for full retirement at 60 with zero tax on investment income. Annual audit: clean. Professional advisory cost: $4,500/year.

Michael: The Investor Who Thought He Was Smarter

Michael was a technology entrepreneur. He had made money quickly in his career and had developed a conviction that high-risk, high-return investments were the path to wealth. He was not interested in ETFs. He was interested in 'edge.'

His $1,000,000 allocation: $500,000 in a fifty-percent shareholding in his own unlisted technology startup (which he valued at $1,000,000, making the SMSF a 50% owner for $500,000); $300,000 in a residential property in Sydney's Western Suburbs, leased to his adult son at $450 per week (market rate: $650 per week); $200,000 in a friend's technology company, based on the friend's promise of 10% annual returns.

Michael's justifications were internally coherent. He knew his startup better than anyone — the SMSF was investing in a business he controlled. His son was a tenant who paid 'reasonable' rent. His friend's company was a genuine opportunity that ETF investors couldn't access.

The subsequent 14 months featured four separate collapses.

October 2024: The friend's technology company failed. ATO investigations were opened in three jurisdictions. Michael's $200,000 was gone. Legal costs pursuing recovery: $50,000. Recovery: nil.

March 2025: ATO data-matching identified the residential property tenancy. Market rental comparison: $650 per week. Michael's rent: $450 per week — 30% below market. Determination: non-arm's length income (NALI). All rental income permanently taxed at 45%. Disposal order issued.

June 2025: Auditor review of the startup shareholding. The single unlisted entity represented 50% of the SMSF's assets. The SIS Act requires that in-house assets — investments in or loans to related parties, or assets leased to related parties — not exceed 5% of the fund's total assets. Where the startup company was a related party (for example, where Michael was a significant shareholder or director), the investment would be an in-house asset. The auditor determined that a related-party relationship existed. Disposal order issued: reduce exposure to below 5% within 90 days.

Michael found an external buyer for the unlisted shares at $350,000 — a loss of $150,000 on his $500,000 purchase. The market for stakes in pre-revenue technology startups is not forgiving when the seller is under regulatory compulsion.

> **$1,000,000 → $230,000**
> **Michael's SMSF: 77% reduction in 3 years**
>
> Friend's company: $200,000 loss. Unlisted shares: $150,000 forced sale loss. Property loss on disposal: $20,000. NALI tax: $35,000. Penalties: $28,560. Legal fees: $86,000. Total: $519,560 in direct losses and costs.

The three-way comparison makes the stakes visceral:

	Robert	Sarah	Michael
Starting balance	$1,000,000	$1,000,000	$1,000,000
Three-year value	$300,000	$1,385,000	$230,000
Strategy	Related-party transactions	Compliant diversified portfolio	Rule-bending high risk
Compliance status	Non-complying, banned trustee	Fully compliant	Multiple breaches
Lesson	Rules are red lines	Compliance enables growth	Cleverness isn't wisdom

Iron Law One: The Sole Purpose Test (Section 62)

We covered the Sole Purpose Test in detail in Chapter Three. Here, we examine its investment-specific application through Helen's holiday property case — a situation where a financially sensible investment strategy was rendered fatally non-compliant by a single, irreversible decision about personal use.

Helen's $108,800 Lesson: 11% Personal Use = 100% Non-Compliance

Helen was 52, an accountant, with $800,000 in her SMSF. In 2023, she had identified a Gold Coast beachfront apartment for $600,000. The property would be used as a short-term rental — Airbnb and direct bookings — for most of the year. On occasional weekends and during school holidays, Helen and her family would use it.

'11% personal use,' she calculated. '89% investment use. The primary purpose is clearly investment.'

Her accountant tried to stop her. Helen proceeded.

The usage record for the first year: short-term rental income from 120 days, generating $37,000. Helen and family personal use: 41 days. Vacant: 204 days.

In October 2024, the ATO review arrived. The evidence was overwhelming: Airbnb records showing Helen had manually blocked 41 days as 'unavailable'; neighbour testimony about frequent weekend appearances; her daughter's Instagram photos from a birthday party at the apartment; utility records showing higher consumption during the blocked periods.

> **The ATO's 'All or Nothing' Ruling**
>
> *"Ms Helen, the Sole Purpose Test requires that your SMSF be maintained 'solely for' retirement benefits — not 'primarily for.' The proportion of personal use is not the test. The existence of any personal use is the test.*
>
> *"Analogy: A restaurant that calls itself a 'vegetarian restaurant' cannot have 1% of its menu containing meat. The description 'solely for retirement benefits' cannot accommodate 1% personal enjoyment.*
>
> *"Your fund has failed the Sole Purpose Test. You have 90 days to dispose of the asset or restore full compliance."*

Helen sold under the ninety-day deadline. The property, which had appreciated from $600,000 to $680,000, sold in a rushed sale for $620,000 — $60,000 below market value because buyers could see the urgency. Direct capital loss: $90,000. NALI tax on the $37,000 rental income: $16,650. Administrative penalties: $21,420. Legal fees: $15,000. Opportunity cost compared to ETF investment: $64,000.

Total: $143,000 lost, plus a five-year ATO monitoring flag.

$143,070 Helen's direct losses (monitoring costs shown separately)

Capital loss on forced sale: $90,000. NALI tax: $16,650. Penalties: $21,420. Legal fees: $15,000. Five-year enhanced monitoring at $5,000/year: $25,000. Helen's reflection: 'SMSF money is future-me's money. It is not current-me's money to enjoy on weekends. That distinction cost me $143,000 to fully understand.'

Iron Law Two: The Related Party Asset Prohibition (Section 66)

Section 66 of the SIS Act is one of the most absolute provisions in the entire SIS Act framework. It prohibits an SMSF from acquiring assets from 'related parties' — defined very broadly to include members, their relatives (including spouses, parents, and siblings), companies controlled by members, and trusts controlled by members.

The prohibition has three narrow exceptions: listed securities at market value, qualifying commercial real property at market value, and business real property transferred by members at market value. Outside these 3 categories, any acquisition from a related party is illegal — regardless of how fair the price is, how independent the valuation was, or how carefully the transaction was structured.

The 3 cases that follow collectively demonstrate a truth about Section 66 that every trustee should understand: creative circumvention schemes consistently fail, often at enormous cost.

Case A: David's 'Temporary Withdrawal' — $352,560

David was 55 and owned one 100% of a manufacturing company with annual revenue of $5 million. In 2023, his company needed $500,000 urgently for capacity expansion. Bank loan approval was delayed.

David's SMSF held $1,200,000. He had an idea.

His accountant refused immediately: 'Section 66 prohibits SMSF from purchasing assets from related parties. Your company is a related party. Not possible.'

David paid $8,000 for a second opinion from an 'aggressive' tax lawyer. The lawyer designed a scheme: David would resign as trustee on 1 July; the SMSF (now with only his wife Sarah as trustee) would purchase a 10%shareholding in his company for $500,000 on 15 July; David would rejoin the SMSF in January 2024. The logic: at the moment of purchase, David was not an SMSF member, so his company was not a related party.

The scheme was executed. The company received its $500,000.

The ATO's review in September 2024 was methodical and unsparing. The ATO cited Part IVA of the Income Tax Assessment Act — the general anti-avoidance provisions — in addition to Section 66. The finding: the temporary resignation was a scheme designed to circumvent a legislative prohibition. The substance of the transaction was a related-party acquisition. The form — the temporary resignation — was disregarded.

Additional finding: even during the period when David was nominally not a trustee, he remained a member and de facto controller of the SMSF. The ATO applied the 'associates' definition broadly to capture this reality.

> **$352,560 David's Section 66 circumvention scheme — total cost**
>
> ATO penalties for s66 breach: $19,800. Back-taxation (non-complying fund status): $28,560. Legal fees defending scheme: $45,000 (including the $8,000 initial advice that created the problem). Company shares (now worth $380K vs $500K paid, following valuation review): $120,000 loss. Tax professional penalties: $139,200 (recoverable from the

> lawyer but destroyed the relationship). Total attributable to David: $352,560.

Case B: Emma's 'Buy-Then-Sell' — $185,000

Emma was 58 and owned a retail business that held commercial property in her company's name. She wanted the SMSF to own the property — a legitimate strategy under the commercial real property exception to Section 66. However, she did not want to sell the property directly from the company to the SMSF, because the stamp duty and CGT implications were significant.

Her solution: the company would first sell the property to an unrelated third party — her accountant — who would then sell it to the SMSF the following week. By going through an intermediary, the acquisition was not 'from a related party.'

The ATO's analysis under Part IVA was straightforward: the interposition of an intermediary was a device designed to circumvent Section 66. The substance of the transaction was a related-party acquisition. The form — the brief intermediary ownership — was a legal fiction. The transaction was treated as a direct related-party acquisition for Section 66 purposes.

Emma's cost: $185,000 in penalties, additional tax liability, and legal fees.

Case C: Tom's 'Buy Back Later' — $319,000

Tom owned shares in his private company and wanted to transfer them to his SMSF. His company was unlisted, meaning the transfer was not eligible for the listed securities exception. His adviser suggested that Tom sell the shares to an unrelated investor, wait 6 months, and then have the SMSF purchase them from the unrelated investor.

Tom and the unrelated investor entered into a side agreement guaranteeing that the investor would sell back to the SMSF at a fixed price after 6 months. The ATO obtained a copy of this agreement during its audit. The determination: the pre-arranged buy-back agreement meant that the unrelated investor was never the beneficial owner of the shares. The transaction was a scheme. The SMSF's acquisition was, in substance, a direct acquisition from Tom.

Tom's cost: $319,000 in penalties, restructuring costs, and forced sale losses.

> **The Section 66 Pattern**
>
> Three different schemes. Three different lawyers or advisers. Three different transaction structures. One outcome: detected, disallowed, and severely penalised.
>
> The Part IVA anti-avoidance provisions give the ATO and courts a broad power to disregard transactions that are entered into primarily for the purpose of obtaining a tax or superannuation benefit. They are specifically designed to prevent exactly the kinds of circumvention schemes we have examined.
>
> The practical lesson: if your strategy involves temporary resignations, intermediary buyers, pre-arranged buy-back agreements, or any other mechanism designed to make a related-party transaction appear to be an arm's-length transaction, it will almost certainly fail. The cost of failing is far greater than the cost of finding a compliant alternative.

Iron Law Three: The Lending Prohibition (Section 65)

Section 65 of the SIS Act prohibits an SMSF trustee from lending money, or giving financial assistance, to a member or a member's relative. This prohibition is broader than it might appear — 'financial assistance' extends beyond formal loans to include guarantees, indemnities, and any arrangement that reduces the financial risk or burden on a member or their family.

Paul's $290,700 Lesson: Helping a Daughter with a Startup

Paul was 62 and had spent his career in property development. His SMSF held $900,000, carefully accumulated over 30 years. In 2022, his ten-7-year-old daughter Sophie established a technology consulting business. She had talent, a few early clients, and an acute shortage of working capital.

Paul's solution seemed elegant. His SMSF would purchase a $200,000 debenture from Sophie's company — effectively lending it $200,000 at a 6% annual interest rate. This was, he reasoned, a legitimate investment: the SMSF would earn 6% interest, Sophie's company would get working capital, and the debenture was secured against the company's intellectual property assets.

His accountant noted the problem immediately. Sophie's company was Sophie's company — and Sophie was Paul's daughter. Section 65 does not permit lending to a member's relative, regardless of the structure, the interest rate, the security, or the commercial rationale. The prohibition is absolute.

Paul proceeded anyway. His reasoning: 'Sophie is a businesswoman. This is a commercial transaction, not a personal gift. The SMSF will earn proper interest. Where is the harm?'

The ATO's Section 65 Position

The harm, as the ATO explained in its review of Paul's fund, is structural. The prohibition exists because the SMSF is supposed to be maintained solely for the benefit of its members in retirement. Any arrangement that directs the fund's resources toward current benefits for members or their families — regardless of how it is structured — compromises that purpose.

The fact that the loan was made at market interest rates, secured by genuine collateral, and documented in a formal

> debenture agreement was irrelevant. The identity of the borrower was the issue.
>
> Section 65 contains no exceptions and no de minimis provision. A one-dollar loan to a member is as prohibited as a one-million-dollar loan.

Sophie's company struggled. By 2023, it had become clear that the consulting model was not working at scale. The company was restructured, shedding most of its contracts and staff. When the ATO review arrived in March 2024, Paul's SMSF held a $200,000 debenture in a company worth approximately $120,000. But the problem was not the investment's value — it was its existence.

The ATO's findings: Section 65 breach; fund deemed non-complying for 2022-23 and 2023-24; back-taxation at 45%; administrative penalties; disposal order.

The disposal of the debenture — now effectively worth the underlying company's assets — recovered $85,000 against the $200,000 investment. Capital loss: $115,000. Back-taxation on 2 years of fund income: $62,000. Penalties: $19,800. Legal fees: $45,000. Interest: $48,900.

> **$290,700 Paul's Section 65 breach — total cost**
>
> Loan recovery: $85,000 against $200,000 invested. Capital loss: $115,000. Back-taxation: $62,000. Penalties: $19,800. Legal fees: $45,000. Additional costs: $48,900. Paul's reflection: 'I was trying to help my daughter. Instead, I damaged both of us. If I had simply given her $200,000 as a personal gift — from my savings, not the SMSF — she would have had the money, my SMSF would be intact, and I would have saved $90,000 in penalties and legal costs.'

Iron Law Four: The Investment Strategy Requirement (Section 52B)

We have discussed the investment strategy requirement in Chapter Three as a compliance obligation. Here, we examine it as an investment discipline tool — and what happens when it is absent.

Lisa's $85,000 Lesson: The Strategy-Free Investment

Lisa was 49, a marketing executive, with an SMSF balance of $600,000. In 2022, she received a tip from a well-connected colleague about a promising technology company about to complete a Series B funding round. The opportunity was time-sensitive — the window was 3 weeks. Lisa committed $200,000 from her SMSF.

She did not consult her adviser before making the commitment. She did not update her investment strategy to reflect the new holding. She did not check whether a single unlisted company investment of this size was consistent with the fund's existing strategy, which specified 'diversification across at least four asset classes,' nor did she consider whether the company was a related party that could create in-house asset exposure.

The technology company performed adequately — it did not collapse or defraud anyone. But Lisa's ATO audit, conducted in 2024, identified multiple compliance failures arising from the investment. Her fund's auditor had flagged the issues but Lisa had not addressed them within the required timeframe.

The investment strategy had never been updated to include the unlisted company. The fund had no documented rationale for the investment. The concentration of $200,000 in a single unlisted entity — representing 33% of the fund's assets — was inconsistent with the existing strategy's diversification requirement, and the absence of documentation made it impossible for the trustees to demonstrate genuine consideration of the investment.

The consequences: penalties for failure to maintain and give effect to the investment strategy ($14,280); penalties for late audit rectification ($6,660); required SMSF trustee education course ($1,500); additional accounting fees for strategy reconstruction ($8,500). When the Series B company's valuation declined in 2023 and Lisa sold the holding at a loss, the direct investment loss was $54,000.

> **$85,000 Lisa's investment-strategy failure — total losses**
>
> Investment loss on Series B stake: $54,000. Penalties: $14,280 + $6,660. Education and reconstruction costs: $10,000. Total: $84,940. The investment was not fraudulent. The company was not a sham. The problem was entirely procedural — a failure to maintain the documentation that gives trustees the framework for making decisions responsibly.

Iron Law Five: The In-House Asset Rule (Section 71)

A common and serious misreading of the SIS Act is the belief that there is a general "5% cap" on any single investment. There is not. The SIS Act does not impose a blanket investment concentration limit. An SMSF can lawfully hold 80% or even 90% of its assets in a single commercial property — provided the investment strategy addresses diversification and liquidity as required under s 52B and Reg 4.09.

What section 71 of the SIS Act does impose is a 5% cap on "in-house assets." This is a defined term. In-house assets broadly captures 3 categories: loans to related parties or related trusts; investments in related-party entities or related trusts; and assets subject to a lease or lease arrangement with a related party — unless a specific exception applies (such as certain business real property leasing arrangements that satisfy the relevant conditions).

The practical rule is this: the total market value of all in-house assets of the SMSF must not exceed 5% of the fund's total assets at any point in time, and is formally tested at 30 June each year. If the fund exceeds the 5% threshold at 30 June, the trustees must formulate and implement a written plan to reduce the in-house asset exposure back below the limit — a process commonly associated with the obligations under s82 of the SIS Act.

The critical point is that the in-house asset rule is triggered by the nature of the counterparty — related or unrelated — not by the size of the position. Concentration risk in the broader portfolio sense (putting too much into one asset class or one property) is addressed through a different mechanism: the investment strategy obligation under s 52B and the requirement to consider diversification and liquidity. These are separate regimes with separate consequences.

Mark's $420,000 Lesson: The Related Party Trap

Mark was a construction company owner with $850,000 in his SMSF. In January 2021, he purchased a $650,000 commercial warehouse in Western Sydney's logistics precinct using an LRBA — $300,000 in SMSF equity and a $350,000 bank loan. The warehouse was leased to an unrelated logistics company at $66,000 per year.

His accountant, Susan, raised two concerns before the purchase. First, $650,000 represented 76%of the SMSF's gross assets — a severe concentration that would make the fund acutely vulnerable to any single event affecting the property or its tenant. The fund's own written investment strategy explicitly required "minimum diversification across three asset classes." Under s 52B and Reg 4.09, trustees must formulate, review, and give effect to a strategy that considers diversification and liquidity. A single warehouse would make it very difficult to show the strategy was being followed in substance. Second, Susan was careful to clarify that the "5% rule" was not triggered by the warehouse purchase itself — the 5% cap under s71 applies to in-house assets, meaning loans to or investments in related parties, or assets leased to related parties. Unless a related party became involved, the in-house asset rule would not apply.

Mark dismissed both concerns. The tenant was a well-established logistics company. The lease had 5 years remaining. Western Sydney logistics property was one of the most reliable asset classes in the country.

He was right about the asset class in general. He was wrong about this specific asset, in this specific timeframe, under these specific financial conditions.

In March 2023, the tenant — Logistics Express Pty Ltd — entered administration. In a single day, the SMSF's entire rental income went to zero. But the loan repayment of $4,200 per month and property expenses of $1,500 per month continued on schedule. For 4 months, the fund lost $5,700 per month in net outflows — $22,800 direct — before Mark found a replacement tenant.

The replacement tenant, sourced through Mark's construction company connections, turned out to be a related party under the SIS Act's broad definition. This created two distinct legal problems Susan had warned about. First, the rent was 14% below market. Where an SMSF enters into non-commercial arrangements with a related party, the income can be assessed as non-arm's length income (NALI) and taxed at the top rate — 45% — permanently on that asset. Second, under an LRBA structure, leasing the LRBA-held property to a related party can cause the SMSF's interest in the holding trust to be classified as an in-house asset under s 71 — unless the relevant exceptions (such as the business real property conditions) are satisfied. Mark had now triggered exactly the in-house asset exposure that Susan had warned about. With the fund's total assets at approximately $800,000 at the time, even a modest valuation of the LRBA interest could push the in-house asset ratio well above the 5% cap.

Then the interest rate cycle turned. The LRBA loan rate rose from 3.5% to 6.5%. Monthly repayments increased from $1,750 to $2,600. Annual interest cost increased by $10,200.

Then the market turned. The warehouse — revalued at $720,000 in late 2022 — was independently revalued at $580,000 in late 2023. A $140,000 decline.

By 2024, the fund was running at a monthly deficit. Mark sold the warehouse in a distressed sale for $530,000 — $50,000 below its already-depressed valuation, and $120,000 below its peak.

The total loss analysis was comprehensive and painful:

Category	Amount	Detail
Capital loss	$172,000	Total acquisition $683K vs net sales proceeds $511K
Vacancy losses	$22,000	4 months at $5,700/month net outflow
Below-market rent	$14,400	18 months × $800/month shortfall
NALI excess tax	$8,100	Tax at 45% vs 15% on NALI income
Interest rate increase	$20,400	Additional annual cost × 3 years proportional
Penalties + legal	$43,300	Strategy breach + arm's-length breach + professional fees
Opportunity cost	$139,800	Conservative: $300K in diversified ETF at 7% × 3 years
TOTAL	$420,000	The complete cost of the related party trap

> **Mark's Reflection**
>
> *"I made the error every property devotee eventually commits — treating belief as analysis. 'Property always appreciates' may be true for the Australian market over 30 years. It is not true for one specific warehouse during one specific three-year window.*
>
> *"I wagered $300,000 of my own capital plus $350,000 of borrowed money on a single building. That was not investment. That was gambling with my retirement.*
>
> *"The most ironic part: Susan told me explicitly that the 5% rule was not the problem with the warehouse purchase. The in-house asset rule would only bite if I brought in a related party. Then I went and brought in a related party. The very risk she had identified — in-house asset exposure under the LRBA — is exactly what I triggered. I dismissed the warning, then walked straight into it.*
>
> *"“Susan was right. I was wrong. $420,000 is the cost of ignoring a specific, correct warning about a specific legal rule."*

Iron Law Six: The Collectibles Rules (Regulation 13.18AA)

SIS Regulation 13.18AA imposes six specific restrictions on SMSF investment in 'collectibles and personal use assets' — a category that includes artworks, jewellery, antiques, coins, stamps, rare books, memorabilia, wine and spirits, motor vehicles, and recreational vessels. These restrictions exist because these assets share a property that makes them fundamentally problematic for SMSF investment: the temptation of personal enjoyment.

Andrew's $180,000 Lesson: The Classic Mustang

Andrew was a senior partner at a Melbourne law firm, 55 years old, with a $1,500,000 SMSF that had always been impeccably managed:

60% blue-chip equities, ten-5% bonds, 15% cash. He had been a model SMSF trustee for a decade.

Within him, however, lived the dream of a 16-year-old boy who had watched Steve McQueen drive a Highland Green Ford Mustang GT Fastback through San Francisco traffic on a cinema screen in 1975. In early 2021, at a Melbourne classic car exhibition, Andrew found that exact car — a 1967 Mustang GT Fastback, Highland Green, V8 engine, 45,000 original miles, near-immaculate condition. Asking price: $180,000.

Andrew did what lawyers do: he researched the rules. He reviewed Regulation 13.18AA and prepared a compliance checklist. Insurance within 7 days: fine, he would arrange it. No use by associates: absolutely, he would not drive it. Storage not at associate residence: he would engage professional storage. Written storage documentation: he was a lawyer, documentation was his strength.

On April 5, 2021, the SMSF purchased the Mustang for $180,000.

The First Compromise: Insurance

Following settlement, Andrew was consumed by a major international arbitration matter. The insurance company call was deferred. Then deferred again. Insurance was activated on day fourteen — 7 days past the regulatory deadline. The regulation specified seven calendar days, not seven business days.

Andrew noted the miss but reassured himself: 'The car is in storage, untouched. This technical irregularity is not something the ATO would pursue.'

It was Andrew's first misapplication of his legal expertise to his SMSF circumstances. He was used to courts that distinguish between material and technical violations. Regulation 13.18AA does not make that distinction.

The Slow Erosion: Personal Use

The Mustang sat in professional storage for 3 months. Then the Melbourne Classic Car Club announced its annual exhibition. Andrew could not resist. He drove it himself — 18 kilometres from storage to the exhibition venue. Justified as 'asset management activity to enhance valuation.'

In September 2021: a retirement gathering for a law firm partner. Andrew drove the Mustang, showing the old colleague the car. 'Just once. A personal moment.'

In December 2021: his son's wedding. The Mustang served as the bridal car. Andrew recorded $500 as 'rental income' in the SMSF accounts, believing the payment legitimised the use. It did not.

Throughout 2022: three classic car exhibitions, one charity display, monthly 'inspection and engine start' sessions. Each use had its own rationalisation. Law, as Andrew well knew, does not consider rationalisation.

The Storage Compromise

In July 2022, the professional storage facility announced a fee increase to $550 per month. Andrew had an empty, climate-controlled, security-alarmed home garage that he had spent $15,000 fitting out — arguably superior to commercial storage. He moved the car home.

His reasoning: a garage is a separate structure from the residence. It should not constitute associate residence.

The ATO's definition of associate residence is unambiguous: it encompasses residential property and all structures on that land, including garages and sheds. Andrew's garage, however independent or luxurious, was part of his home property.

The 2023 Audit: Everything Surfaces

Auditor Rachel had 10 years of SMSF experience. Her review of the Mustang compliance was methodical. The evidence she assembled was, for Andrew, mortifying:

Andrew's Instagram — multiple photographs of him beside the Mustang at exhibition venues and at his son's wedding. The odometer — 45,000 miles at purchase, now 45,380 miles, with every mile on a collectible-grade classic being a documented reduction in value. The wedding photographer's official website — high-resolution images of the Mustang as the bridal car. The law firm's website — a retirement announcement mentioning 'Andrew's classic Mustang.' The utility records from his home garage showing power consumption consistent with climate-control equipment. The exhibition organisers' records showing the Mustang as a registered entry, with Andrew as the nominated driver.

$180,000 Andrew's collectibles compliance failure — total cost

Penalties (sole purpose + insurance + use + storage violations): $39,600. Asset loss (purchased $180K, sold to self at independent valuation $160K): $20,000. Insurance (8 years): $8,000. Storage costs: $5,600. Transport and miscellaneous: $1,200. Legal fees (ATO response): $25,000. Additional audit fees: $5,000. Five-year enhanced monitoring: $25,000. Additional costs: $51,600. TOTAL: approximately $180,000.

The Irony Andrew Identified

"Had I purchased that Mustang personally — with my own savings, not the SMSF — I could have driven it whenever I wished, kept it in my garage, used it for my son's wedding. All perfectly legal. No SMSF violation. The tax savings I was chasing through the SMSF structure amounted to a few thousand dollars over the ownership period.

"To capture those tax savings, I incurred $180,000 in penalties and losses.

> *"SMSF is a retirement savings vehicle, not a hobby storage facility. If you want to enjoy something — drive it, wear it, drink it, display it — buy it personally. SMSF assets you may not touch. This is not a grey area."*

Chapter Four Summary: The Six Iron Laws

Rule	Section	Prohibition	Key Case	Cost
Sole Purpose	s62	No personal use, no current benefits	Helen's holiday property	$143,000
Related Party Assets	s66	Cannot buy assets from related parties (3 narrow exceptions)	David's circumvention scheme	$352,560
Lending Prohibition	s65	Cannot lend to members or relatives	Paul's daughter's startup	$290,700
Investment Strategy	s52B	Written strategy required; must be followed	Lisa's undocumented investment	$85,000
In-House Asset Limit	s71	Related-party exposure max 5% (in-house assets)	Mark's related party tenant mistake	$420,000

Collectibles	Reg 13.18AA	6 locks: insurance, use, storage, documentation	Andrew's Mustang	$180,000

Cumulative cost across 8 cases: $1,974,000. Average cost per case: $246,750.

In every single case, the trustee believed they understood the rules. In every single case, a qualified SMSF adviser, asked in advance, would have identified the problem and prevented the loss. In some cases the adviser did identify the problem and was overridden. In others, the trustee never asked.

The next chapter examines the tax architecture of an SMSF — the extraordinary wealth-building opportunity available to those who navigate it correctly, and the equally extraordinary destruction available to those who do not.

The In-House Asset Test: 5% That Can Trigger Much More

The in-house asset limit — the rule that no more than 5% of an SMSF's assets may consist of loans to or investments in related parties — is one of the more technically specific rules in the SMSF framework. It is also one that can be inadvertently breached through normal fund operations, without the trustee having made any deliberate related party transaction.

Consider a fund that holds a 5% investment in a unit trust that is not controlled by the trustees — this would qualify as a non-related party investment. But if, several years later, the trustees acquire additional units in that trust through a new investment, and those additional units take their total holding above 50%, the trust becomes a controlled entity and therefore a related party. The investment that was previously permissible is now an in-house asset. The 5% limit has been breached not through a new transaction but through a change in the classification of an existing holding.

The remedy when a breach occurs — whether through a deliberate decision or an inadvertent classification change — is a disposal obligation: the fund must reduce its in-house asset exposure to below 5% within 12 months. If the in-house assets cannot be liquidated within that period, the fund must submit a written plan to the ATO for remediation. Failure to remediate is a registrable contravention.

Scenario	In-House Asset Classification	Risk Level
Loan to member's wholly owned company	Definite in-house asset; 5% cap applies immediately	High
Investment in unit trust where trustee holds 25% of units	Depends on whether trustee is an 'associate' — analysis required	Medium
Investment in listed company where member is a director	Not in-house asset if held for investment purposes, not because of the relationship	Low
Rent deferred on commercial property to related party for 3 months	Potentially in-house asset (deferred rent can be characterised as a loan)	Medium-High
Investment in a private company where member's adult child is a director	Potentially related party — 'associate' analysis required	Medium

Investment Strategy Review: What the ATO Actually Expects

The requirement to have a written investment strategy is not satisfied by producing a document that says 'the fund will invest in shares and property.' The ATO has published specific guidance on what a compliant investment strategy must contain, and the standard is materially higher than many trustees appreciate.

A compliant investment strategy must: be tailored to the specific circumstances of the fund and its members; address each of the five required considerations (risk, return, liquidity, diversification, and insurance); be consistent with the fund's actual investment decisions; be reviewed and updated when material changes occur; and be documented in a way that demonstrates genuine consideration of each of the required elements.

The ATO's 2019 letter campaign — in which it wrote directly to thousands of SMSF trustees whose investment strategies appeared to be generic templates — was a signal of the regulator's intention to enforce this standard. Trustees who received those letters and simply updated their template without engaging with the substance of their actual investment approach were, in my view, missing the point. The investment strategy is meant to be a genuine record of the trustees' investment thinking, not a compliance document that is filed and forgotten.

The Insurance Consideration: Often Missing, Always Required

The investment strategy must specifically address whether the trustees have considered insurance for each member of the fund. This does not mean that insurance must be held — it means that the question must have been specifically considered and the outcome documented. If the trustees have determined that insurance is not necessary or appropriate for a specific member, the strategy must explain why.

In practice, I find that approximately 60% of investment strategies I review do not adequately address the insurance consideration. They contain a generic statement that 'insurance has been considered' without any member-specific analysis. This is not compliant in my view. The insurance consideration must be specific to each member: what coverage does this member need, what coverage do they currently hold (inside and outside superannuation), and how does the trustees' investment strategy position the fund to meet insurance obligations?

The investment strategy audit is an annual opportunity to ensure that this analysis is genuinely current. A member who was adequately insured at age 45 with a $3 million mortgage and two dependent children may be over-insured or under-insured at55 when the mortgage is paid off and the children are independent. The strategy review should track these lifecycle changes and document the trustees' updated assessment.

Concentration Risk: The Portfolio That Isn't Diversified

The SIS Act's investment strategy requirement includes specific consideration of diversification — the spreading of investments across asset classes, sectors, and geographies to reduce the risk of material loss from any single exposure. The requirement does not mandate any particular level of diversification, but it does require that the trustees have genuinely considered it and documented their approach.

I want to address a specific and common form of concentration risk that I see in SMSF portfolios: the single-property fund. Many trustees establish an SMSF specifically to purchase a direct property — typically a commercial property under an LRBA. The property may represent 75% to 90% of the fund's total assets. The investment strategy typically contains a paragraph explaining that the trustees are aware of the concentration risk but have determined that the specific property provides sufficient return to justify the concentration.

This is a legally permissible position. It is also, from a pure portfolio management perspective, a significant risk. A property portfolio of one asset is exposed to: the specific risks of that property's location (infrastructure changes, demographic shifts, commercial precinct deterioration); the specific risks of that property's tenant (tenancy vacancy, tenant insolvency, rent default); the specific risks of the LRBA structure (interest rate changes, bank covenant requirements); and the liquidity risk of needing to sell the property to meet cash obligations (minimum pension payments, insurance premiums, operating costs).

The case of Mark and the warehouse in Chapter Four's main text — $420,000 in losses from a single property with a failed tenant and an interest rate that doubled — is the illustration of what happens when these risks materialise simultaneously. The fund had no other assets of substance to draw on. The only exit was a distressed sale.

Diversification is not a sacrifice of return. Across financial cycles, diversified portfolios have consistently produced better risk-adjusted returns than concentrated ones. The illusion of diversification through a single high-quality asset is a comfort that the market tests with unsettling regularity.

The LRBA Deep Dive

Limited Recourse Borrowing Arrangements — The Most Powerful Tool in the SMSF Toolkit, Used Correctly

No single feature of the SMSF structure attracts more attention — from trustees, from financial promoters, from regulators, and from the financial media — than the Limited Recourse Borrowing Arrangement. The LRBA is the mechanism by which an SMSF can borrow money to acquire an asset, using that asset as security, while limiting the lender's recourse to the acquired asset itself. It is, when used correctly and in the right circumstances, a genuinely powerful wealth-building tool. It is, when used incorrectly or in unsuitable circumstances, a mechanism for accelerating financial losses.

This section is dedicated to the LRBA in the depth it deserves. We will cover the legal structure, the types of assets that can be acquired, the commercial and related-party lending distinctions, the specific cash flow requirements, the tax treatment, and — critically — the risk profile that makes an LRBA appropriate for some trustees and genuinely dangerous for others.

The Legal Architecture of the LRBA: The Bare Trust Structure

The fundamental legal constraint on SMSF borrowing is straightforward: the SMSF cannot hold an asset subject to a charge or encumbrance. If the SMSF borrows and uses the borrowed funds to buy an asset, the lender would normally take security over that asset by registering a charge against it. But a charge against an SMSF asset is prohibited under the SIS Act.

The LRBA circumvents this prohibition through a legal structure called the bare trust (also known as a holding trust, custodian trust, or security trust). The arrangement works as follows: the borrowed funds are used by a separate bare trust to acquire the asset. The bare trust holds legal title to the asset. The SMSF holds beneficial ownership — the right to occupy the economic benefits of the asset. The lender takes security over the bare trust's interest in the asset. The SMSF's other assets are not available to the lender, hence the 'limited recourse' description.

The bare trust must be a separate legal entity from the SMSF. It requires its own trust deed, its own trustee (typically a corporate entity), its own bank account for the rental income, and its own registration. Establishing the bare trust correctly is critical — an improperly structured bare trust can invalidate the entire LRBA, potentially triggering both a SIS Act breach and significant adverse tax consequences.

> **The LRBA Legal Structure — Four Parties**
>
> 1. SMSF (beneficial owner of the asset — holds the economic interest) 2. Bare Trust (legal owner of the asset — holds title, provides security to lender) 3. Bare Trustee (typically a corporate trustee — manages the bare trust) 4. Lender (bank or related party — provides the finance; recourse limited to the asset) When the loan is fully repaid, the legal title transfers from the bare trust to the SMSF directly.

What Assets Can Be Acquired via LRBA?

The SIS Act allows LRBAs to be used to acquire 'acquirable assets' — a defined category that includes most standard investment assets but excludes certain high-risk or speculative assets. The key requirement is that the asset be a 'single acquirable asset' — one asset or a collection of identical assets that together form a single holding.

This 'single asset' requirement has been interpreted with some specificity. A single parcel of land is a single acquirable asset. A collection of identical shares (one hundred BHP shares purchased in one transaction) is a single acquirable asset. A building and the land on which it sits are a single acquirable asset. But two separate parcels of land purchased in a single transaction are not a single acquirable asset — they are two assets that each require separate LRBA structures.

Asset Type	LRBA Permitted?	Notes
Commercial property	Yes	Most common LRBA asset; related party (business real property) rules apply if purchased from related party
Residential investment property	Yes	Cannot be purchased from related party; cannot be used by member or associates
Listed shares (single company, one parcel)	Yes	Less common; margin loan structure often preferred outside super for shares
Listed ETF units (one class, one transaction)	Yes	Single acquirable asset if purchased in one transaction
Unlisted unit trust units	Permitted with restrictions	Complex analysis required; widely held test applies
Business real property from related party	Permitted	Must meet business real property definition and arm's length valuation

Residential property from related party	Prohibited	Cannot acquire residential property from related party under any circumstances
Assets that cannot be valued	Prohibited	LRBA asset must be capable of independent valuation
Assets to be improved	Prohibited during loan period	Asset improvements during the loan period are not permitted; can occur after loan repaid

The 'No Improvement' Rule: What It Means for Property Investment

The prohibition on improving an LRBA asset during the loan period is one of the most practically constraining — and frequently overlooked — features of the LRBA structure. If an SMSF acquires a commercial property via LRBA with the intention of renovating or improving it, those improvements cannot occur until the loan is fully repaid. Any capital expenditure that improves (as opposed to merely maintaining or repairing) the asset during the loan period is a breach.

The distinction between repair and improvement is not always clear-cut. Replacing a deteriorated roof with materials of equivalent quality is maintenance. Replacing a deteriorated roof with materials of higher quality or greater specification is improvement. Repainting a property is maintenance. Extending a property by adding floor space is clearly improvement. The grey areas between these extremes require specific advice before any significant capital expenditure is incurred on an LRBA property.

Trustees who acquire a commercial property via LRBA with a renovation plan should structure the acquisition timeline around the loan repayment: make a larger initial deposit to shorten the loan period, or establish a shorter loan term. The renovation cannot begin until after the title has transferred from the bare trust to the SMSF — which occurs only on full loan repayment.

Commercial Lending vs Related Party Lending: A Critical Distinction

SMSF LRBAs can be funded by either commercial lenders (banks and other authorised deposit-taking institutions) or by related parties (the members themselves, their relatives, or their associated entities). The regulatory requirements for each type of lending are quite different — and the consequences of getting a related party loan wrong are severe.

Commercial SMSF LRBA Lending

Commercial banks that offer SMSF LRBA products typically impose their own due diligence requirements that provide a useful first-pass filter on suitability. They will assess the SMSF's financial position, the members' income and creditworthiness, the property's value and rental potential, and the fund's ability to service the loan from projected rental income and contributions. Banks typically require a minimum deposit of 20% - 30%, and some require evidence of the SMSF's investment strategy addressing the LRBA.

The interest rate on commercial SMSF LRBA products is typically higher than owner-occupier residential lending — reflecting the limited recourse structure and the specialist nature of the product. During the 2022-2025 interest rate cycle, rates of 6% to 8% were common. At 8% interest on a $1,000,000 loan, the annual interest cost is $80,000 — before any principal repayment, before property costs, before maintenance. The property must generate sufficient rental income, combined with other fund income, to cover this cost sustainably.

Related Party LRBA Lending: The Safe Harbour Rules

A related party — including the member themselves, a company they control, or their self-managed superannuation fund's members collectively — can lend money to the SMSF for an LRBA. This is permitted, but it often needs to comply with the ATO's safe harbour rules, which specify the interest rate, loan term, loan-to-value ratio, and other conditions that the arrangement must meet to be treated as arm's length.

The safe harbour interest rate for SMSF LRBA products is published by the ATO annually and is indexed to the Reserve Bank of Australia's Indicator Lending Rates. For residential property, the safe harbour rate is typically aligned with the standard variable rate for housing; for commercial property, it is aligned with a higher indicative commercial rate. The safe harbour loan-to-value ratio is typically 70% both commercial property and residential property.

An SMSF LRBA from a related party that does not comply with the safe harbour terms — where the interest rate is below the safe harbour rate, or the loan term is more favourable than the safe harbour term — is often a non-arm's length arrangement. The income from the LRBA property is assessed as NALI at 45%. The entire rental income from the property, for every year the non-compliant arrangement exists, is assessed at the punitive rate.

> **Permanent Tax at 45% The Related Party LRBA NALI Risk**
>
> A related party loan that does not comply with ATO safe harbour terms often creates permanent NALI contamination on the LRBA property's income. There is no 'fix' after the fact — the non-arm's length income is assessed for every year the property produces income under the non-compliant arrangement.

I have reviewed cases where members lent money to their SMSF at a 'friendly' interest rate significantly below the market rate — believing they were being financially generous to their own retirement fund. The outcome: every dollar of rental income from the property, indefinitely, taxed at 45%. On a property generating $60,000 per year in rent, the additional annual tax cost (compared to the 15% accumulation rate) was $18,000. Over 10 years: $180,000. The 'generosity' was extraordinarily expensive.

The LRBA Cash Flow Analysis: Doing the Numbers Honestly

The most important discipline in evaluating an LRBA opportunity is a thorough cash flow analysis — not the optimistic version that assumes full occupancy and minimal costs, but the stress-tested version that models vacancy periods, interest rate increases, maintenance costs, and the specific profile of the SMSF's other income sources.

Cash Flow Item	Optimistic Assumption	Realistic Stress-Test
Gross rental yield (commercial)	6.5% of property value	5.5% (lower during vacancy; lower in weak markets)
Vacancy rate	0% (no vacancy modelled)	8-12% (1 month per year average)
Property management fee	7% of gross rent	8-9% including administration
Maintenance and repairs	0.5% of property value	1.5% (including irregular large items)

Insurance	$5,000 per year	$6,500-$8,000 (commercial property rates)
Council rates and land tax	$4,000 per year	$5,000-$6,500
Interest cost (7.5% on $800K loan)	$60,000 per year	$60,000 (fixed; increases if rates rise)
Net cash position (on $1.2M property)	Slightly positive	Potentially $15,000 - $25,000 negative cash flow per year

The stress-test reveals that a commercial LRBA property in current market conditions is frequently cash-flow negative — the fund must find additional cash from other sources (contributions, other investments, existing cash holdings) to service the loan. This is not inherently a problem — negative gearing inside superannuation has tax efficiency advantages during the accumulation phase. But it is a structural dependency that must be explicitly planned for. A fund that exhausts its cash reserves servicing the LRBA has no buffer for the minimum pension payments, the annual audit, the insurance premiums, or the unexpected maintenance cost.

The fund's cash flow model should be run in full before an LRBA is committed — not by the real estate agent promoting the property, and not by the mortgage broker seeking to arrange the finance, but by the trustee's independent financial adviser whose role is to identify the risks as well as the opportunities.

The LRBA Exit Strategy: Planning Repayment from Inception

Every LRBA entered into should have a clearly documented exit strategy from inception. How will the loan be repaid? Over what timeline? From what sources? What happens if the property cannot be sold at a price that covers the outstanding loan balance?

The most common LRBA exit strategies are: gradual repayment from fund income (rental income, contributions, investment returns from other assets); lump-sum repayment from a large contribution event (downsizer contribution, sale of assets outside superannuation); sale of the property when the loan is substantially repaid and the capital gain can be taken in pension phase (generating CGT-exempt proceeds); and inheritance or death benefit — where the property passes to a reversionary beneficiary or is sold and distributed as a death benefit.

The critical planning constraint: the LRBA must be fully repaid before the property can be improved, before the title can transfer to the SMSF, and before the fund can be wound up. A fund that plans to wind up in 5 years and holds an LRBA with 10 years remaining must either repay the loan early (from additional contributions, from sale of other assets, or from the property proceeds) or extend the wind-up timeline. This constraint interacts with every other aspect of the fund's lifecycle planning.

The Interest Rate Sensitivity Analysis

SMSF LRBAs are predominantly variable-rate instruments. The experience of the 2022-2025 rate cycle — in which the Reserve Bank increased rates from near-zero to over 4% in less than 2 years — provides a recent and visceral illustration of the interest rate sensitivity of LRBA-dependent SMSF cash flows.

A fund with a $1,200,000 LRBA at a variable rate that increased from 4% to 8% over ten-4 months experienced a doubling of its annual interest cost: from $48,000 to $96,000. If the fund's rental income was $72,000 per year, a fund that had been cash-flow positive at 4% became cash-flow negative at 8%, generating a $24,000 annual shortfall that had to be funded from other sources.

The responsible analysis of an LRBA opportunity includes a sensitivity analysis: what does the fund's cash flow look like at the current interest rate, at 2% above the current rate, and at 4% above the current rate? If the fund cannot sustain the cash flow position at a rate four percentage points above today's rate, the LRBA represents a risk that may not be appropriate for the fund's specific circumstances.

Tax Treatment of LRBA Interest and Deductions

One of the tax advantages of SMSF LRBAs in accumulation phase is the deductibility of interest payments against the fund's taxable income. At a 15% tax rate, a $60,000 annual interest bill produces a tax deduction worth $9,000. This partially offsets the cash cost of the borrowing.

In pension phase, the tax treatment changes. If the LRBA property is in the pension segment (under the segregated ECPI method), the interest is still deductible — but against income that is entirely exempt from tax. The deduction is, in effect, wasted: the fund has no tax liability against which to offset it. This is one of the reasons that LRBAs are most tax-efficient in accumulation phase, and that the timing of pension commencement relative to LRBA repayment requires careful analysis.

The optimal sequence in many cases: repay the LRBA during the accumulation phase, using the interest deductions to reduce the 15% tax burden. Once the loan is fully repaid and the property title transfers to the SMSF, commence the pension. The property, now free of the LRBA structure, is transferred to the pension segment, and any future capital gains on the property are completely exempt from CGT under the ECPI rules.

10 Questions to Ask Before Entering an LRBA

Before committing to a limited recourse borrowing arrangement, every trustee should be able to answer these 10 questions satisfactorily. If you cannot answer any of them — or if the answers are uncomfortable — the LRBA warrants further analysis before proceeding.

Question	What a Good Answer Looks Like
What is the specific investment case for this property?	Documented return expectation, rental yield analysis, capital growth thesis, comparable property transactions
What is the stress-tested cash flow position at interest rates 3% above current?	Fund remains able to meet all obligations including minimum pension, insurance, and maintenance
How will the loan be repaid, and by when?	Specific repayment plan documented in investment strategy; timeline aligned with retirement/wind-up plans
Does the property represent more than 50% of the fund's total assets after acquisition?	If yes, what is the documented basis for accepting this concentration risk?
Is the property a related party transaction, and if so, have the business real property and arm's length requirements been verified?	Written legal opinion confirming compliance; independent valuation obtained
Is the bare trust structure correctly established, with separate trustee, trust deed, and bank account?	Legal confirmation; separate entity register records
Is there sufficient liquidity in the fund to cover a 3-month vacancy period?	Cash or liquid assets sufficient to cover $15,000-$25,000 shortfall for up to 3 months

Has the related party LRBA been assessed against ATO safe harbour terms (if applicable)?	Written confirmation that interest rate, LVR, and loan term comply with safe harbour
Is the fund's insurance strategy updated to cover the LRBA liability?	Life and TPD coverage reviewed; ensures loan can be repaid in event of member death or disability
Has the investment strategy been updated to specifically address the LRBA?	Written investment strategy documents the LRBA, acknowledges concentration risk, and addresses insurance

The LRBA and Retirement Planning: Putting It All Together

When a limited recourse borrowing arrangement is structured correctly — with a compliant bare trust, a commercial or safe harbour-compliant related party loan, a property that meets all the SIS Act requirements, and a fund with sufficient cash flow to service the borrowing through market cycles — it represents one of the most effective wealth-building strategies available within the Australian tax system.

The combination of pre-tax contributions funding the deposit and interest payments (at 15% tax), rental income taxed at 15% in accumulation (or 0% in pension), and eventual capital gain taxed at 0% in pension phase produces a compounded, tax-efficient investment outcome that is not achievable through any other commonly accessible investment structure.

David — the SMSF member in Chapter Two who used an LRBA to acquire a commercial property and arrived at retirement with $3,550,000 compared to the $1,850,000 to $2,150,000 of his retail and industry fund comparators — is not a fictional ideal. He is a composite of real clients who used the LRBA correctly, managed their fund's cash flow prudently, maintained the compliance structure rigorously, and were rewarded with a materially better retirement outcome as a result.

The message is not that every SMSF should have an LRBA. The message is that for trustees who have the balance, the income, the specific investment case, and the professional support to use the LRBA structure correctly, it is an extraordinarily powerful tool — and that tool, like every powerful tool, is most valuable in the hands of someone who understands exactly how it works.

A Final Word on Property in Superannuation: The Liquidity Imperative

Every chapter of this book that touches on property investment in SMSFs — the investment rules, the tax architecture, the insurance blind spot, and this deep dive on LRBAs — returns eventually to the same foundational constraint: property is an illiquid asset in a structure that has mandatory, time-sensitive cash obligations.

The minimum pension requirement does not care whether your SMSF's only liquid asset is a property in a slow market. The insurance premium renewal date does not care whether the fund is cash-flow negative on its LRBA this month. The ATO's compliance deadlines do not adjust for the fact that your term deposit matures next month, not this month.

Managing the liquidity requirements of an SMSF that holds illiquid assets — property above all — requires planning that is as careful and ongoing as the investment strategy itself. My working rule: maintain liquid or near-liquid assets equivalent to at least 18 months of mandatory cash obligations (minimum pension payments, insurance premiums, annual compliance costs, LRBA interest). This is not a precise formula — the specific buffer depends on the fund's income profile, the volatility of its rental income, and the sensitivity of its cash position to interest rate changes. But the principle is constant: illiquid assets in a fund with mandatory cash obligations require a liquidity buffer that the fund can call on when the timing between income and obligation does not align.

The trustees who get this right sleep well. The ones who don't make emergency calls to their advisers in January, discovering that they cannot make the minimum pension payment without selling the property in a market that is not cooperating. The difference between these outcomes is, again, planning. And planning, in this context, means understanding the full cash flow profile of the fund — not just the investment return, but the mandatory obligations — and maintaining the buffer that makes the cash flow profile sustainable across the full range of foreseeable conditions.

It is, in the end, the same principle that runs through every chapter of this book: what you do not plan for will eventually plan for you. Plan deliberately. Seek expert support. Review annually. And give yourself the time to exit well, whatever exit looks like for your specific circumstances.

Chapter Five

The Tax Architecture

Three tax worlds. A $0 paradise and a 45% penalty hell. How to stay in the right one.

The superannuation system exists, in part, because Australian governments have concluded that ordinary market incentives are insufficient to motivate adequate retirement saving. To supplement those incentives, the system provides extraordinary tax concessions. During the accumulation phase, investment earnings are taxed at 15% — a fraction of the rate most high-income earners pay personally. During the pension phase, they are taxed at0. Capital gains on assets held for more than 12 months attract further concessions.

These concessions represent, over a lifetime, a wealth advantage measured in hundreds of thousands of dollars for even a moderately successful investor. For a well-structured SMSF in the hands of a high-income earner with a clear strategy, the lifetime tax advantage can exceed $800,000.

But the tax architecture has a shadow. When an SMSF falls into non-compliance — when a transaction is characterised as non-arm's length, or when the fund is declared non-complying — the same framework that provides a 15% paradise can impose 45% penalty taxation. This is not a marginal difference. It is a 200 percent increase in the tax rate on every dollar of income and gains.

This chapter maps the three tax worlds of an SMSF and the paths between them, through the lens of cases that illuminate both the opportunity and the danger.

Three Tax Worlds: A Complete Map

Tax World	Trigger	Income Tax	Capital Gains	Practical Implication

Accumulation Phase	Fund has active contributions / pre-retirement	15%	10% (if held 12+ months)	Normal operating tax position
Pension Phase (ECPI)	Member commences pension, conditions of release met	0%	0% (completely ignored)	Maximum wealth accumulation
NALI / Non-Complying	Breach detected; non-arm's length transaction	45%	45%	Catastrophic — permanent or multi-year

The journey through these three worlds — and the critical importance of both reaching the pension phase and staying out of the NALI penalty zone — is best understood through Jennifer's complete story.

Jennifer's Three-World Journey

Jennifer Watson, a Sydney specialist physician, established her SMSF in 2019 at age 56 with a transfer of $500,000 from her industry fund and an additional personal contribution of $100,000. Her fund's initial structure: $300,000 in quality Australian shares (a mix of ETFs and blue-chip direct holdings), $100,000 in a commercial property in Chatswood — a small ground-floor office — purchased at $300,000 with a modest LRBA, and $75,000 in cash.

Her adviser set her accumulation phase tax strategy from day one: salary sacrifice the maximum concessional contribution amount each year, maximising the tax saving on her $280,000 income. The strategy was straightforward and effective.

Year One to Three: Accumulation Phase — The Comfort Zone

During her first 3 years, Jennifer's fund operated in the accumulation phase. Every dollar of investment income was taxed at 15%. This was substantially better than Jennifer's marginal personal tax rate of 47%, but it was not yet the optimal position.

Her annual investment income during this period averaged $75,000: rental income from the Chatswood office ($25,000 after LRBA interest), dividends from the share portfolio ($30,000), and interest on cash ($5,000), plus $15,000 in various ETF distributions.

Tax on $75,000 at 15%: $11,250 per year. Tax at Jennifer's personal rate: $35,250 per year. Annual saving: $24,000. Over three accumulation years: $72,000 in total tax savings.

Jennifer was satisfied. She understood that accumulation phase was not the destination — it was the pathway to something better.

Year Four: Pension Phase — Zero Tax

In July 2022, Jennifer turned60. She, as self-employed, choose to cease from being an active physician at the time commencing a pension from her SMSF to access the zero-tax pension phase. She did not have to stop working — once a member has met a condition of release (reaching preservation age and retiring from gainful employment, or turning 60 and ceasing any employment arrangement, or simply turning 65), they can access the pension phase tax concessions regardless of whether they continue to work later on after the pension account was set up.

The mechanics: Jennifer commuted her entire $780,000 SMSF balance into an account-based pension. This took her from accumulation phase (15% tax) to pension phase (0%) in a single transaction.

Her annual investment income for the first full pension phase year: $78,000. Rental income: $28,000. Dividends: $35,000. Interest: $15,000.

Tax on $78,000 in pension phase: zero. Under ECPI — Exempt Current Pension Income — rules, all investment income earned by the SMSF while it is paying a pension to a member is exempt from tax. Capital gains on assets sold while the fund is in pension phase are not only exempt from income tax — under Section 118-320 of the ITAA 1997, they are completely ignored. They do not appear in the fund's tax assessment at all.

> **$78,000 income → $0 tax**
> **Jennifer's pension phase: the zero-tax world**
>
> Rental income $28,000: tax-free. Dividends $35,000: tax-free. Interest $15,000: tax-free. Capital gains on asset sales: completely excluded from assessment. Annual tax saving vs personal income: $36,660. Jennifer's comment: 'I realised I should have retired earlier.'

Jennifer was jubilant. Sitting across the table from her accountant as the first pension-phase tax return was reviewed, she calculated that over 30 years of expected retirement, the pension phase tax saving could exceed $1,000,000.

She did not yet know that her jubilation would be short-lived.

Year Five: NALI — The 45% Penalty Hell

In August 2023, Jennifer's son David — 28 years old, newly self-employed — established a small technology consulting business. He needed an office. The Chatswood property in his mother's SMSF was perfectly located.

She asked David what his budget was. He said $45,000 per year. She checked with the property manager: market rate for comparable commercial space in the area was $60,000 annually. She decided to accept $45,000 — a $15,000 discount to help her son get his business off the ground.

The conversation took approximately 90 seconds. The consequences will persist for the life of the Chatswood property.

The ATO's NALI Analysis

In July 2024, the ATO issued a review notice. The finding was precise and permanent:

> **ATO Review Determination — Jennifer's SMSF**
>
> The Chatswood office rental to David IT Pty Ltd (a company controlled by David, your son — a related party) at $45,000 per annum constitutes Non-Arm's Length Income (NALI) under Section 295-550 of the ITAA 1997.
>
> Market rental assessment: $60,000 per annum. Actual rent: $45,000 per annum. Variance: 25% below market. Tenant: Related party.
>
> Consequences under the 2019 NALI reforms:
>
> 1. 2023-24 rental income of $45,000 is taxed at 45%.
>
> 2. ALL future income from this asset — rent, capital gains, regardless of the identity of any future tenant — is permanently taxed at 45%.
>
> 3. The 45% rate is permanent and irremovable. It follows the asset, not the transaction.
>
> 4. There is no mechanism under current law to restore this asset to its prior tax position.

Jennifer's accountant walked through the implications with the same careful professionalism he always applied, but the numbers were difficult to soften.

For the current year: $45,000 × 45% = $20,250 tax. Previously: zero tax.

For every year the property is held: $20,250+ in annual tax that would otherwise be zero.

On eventual sale: the capital gain on the Chatswood property — currently $300,000 purchase price, likely $500,000 eventual sale price, $200,000 gain — would be taxed at 45%. Tax: $90,000. Previously: zero tax.

Total forward cost of Jennifer's ninety-second rent concession decision: $191,250.

Jennifer asked the question every client in her position asks: 'What can we do to fix it?'

Option	Available?	Outcome
Increase rent to $60,000 market rate immediately	No	NALI is already triggered; future rate irrelevant
Lease to unrelated third party at market rate	No	Stigma follows the asset, not the tenant
Transfer property to another SMSF member	No	Still within the same SMSF
Pay backdated rent to cover the shortfall	No	NALI has already been assessed
Sell the property (crystallise the tax)	Yes	Capital gain $200K at 45% = $90K tax; then buy a clean asset
Hold and pay annual NALI tax	Yes	$20,250+/year until sale

Jennifer chose to hold. She would pay $20,250 per year in tax that should have been zero, until the market offered a good opportunity to sell. She would then absorb the $90,000 capital gains tax, use the proceeds to purchase a different property that had no NALI contamination, and start again.

The cost of the ninety-second conversation: $191,250, spread over years of draining taxation.

> ### $191,250 Jennifer's NALI — cost of a $45,000 kindness
>
> 3 years of rent savings to son: $15,000/year × 3 = $45,000 (estimated). Jennifer's SMSF loss: $191,250 (ongoing tax + eventual CGT). Net family loss: $146,250. Correct approach: gift David $45,000 in cash from personal funds. Legal, tax-efficient, $146,250 cheaper.

ECPI: The Mechanics of Zero Tax

Jennifer's pension phase transition illustrates the most powerful tax mechanism available to SMSF members. But the Exempt Current Pension Income rules are more complex than a simple 'retire and pay zero tax' proposition. There are two pathways to ECPI, each with important differences.

Method One: The Segregated Asset Method

If 100% of a fund's assets are allocated to paying pension liabilities — in other words, all members are fully in pension phase and there are no accumulation accounts — the fund can use the segregated asset method. Under this approach, all investment income is ECPI. Capital gains are not merely exempt — they are completely disregarded. The fund does not even calculate them. Annual simplicity.

The catch: this method requires that the fund maintain 100% pension phase for the entire financial year. Any break — any contribution, any commencement of a new accumulation account, even a single employer contribution on a single day — destroys the entire year's segregated status and forces recalculation under the less favourable unsegregated method.

Tom's Near-Disaster: 5 Days and $5,000

Tom Bradley had executed his SMSF transition to full pension phase perfectly. On 1 July 2023, his entire $1,500,000 moved to pension phase. All income for the 2023-24 year — $90,000 in ordinary income, $170,000 in capital gains — would be zero tax under the segregated method. Total tax liability for the year: zero.

On 26 June 2025 — 5 days before the end of the financial year — Tom accepted a short-term consulting project. The client company paid $5,000 as an employer contribution to Tom's SMSF.

Tom's accountant called in near-panic the next morning. The $5,000 had created an accumulation account. From 26 June to 30 June — 5 days — the fund was no longer one hundred percent pension phase. The segregated method was invalidated for the entire year. The fund needed to recalculate using the unsegregated method.

The good news: because the accumulation contamination affected only 5/365 days, and the accumulation amount ($5,000) was a tiny fraction of the $1,500,000 total, the ECPI percentage under the unsegregated method was 99.995%. Tax liability: $2.10.

Tom was fortunate. The timing was compressed (5 days near year-end) and the amount was small (0.33% of total assets). Had he received the contribution in July instead of June — at the start of the year — the impact would have been dramatic. Had the amount been $200,000 instead of $5,000, the impact would have been significant.

> **The Worst-Case Version of Tom's Mistake**
>
> If Tom had received a $50,000 contribution on 1 July (the first day of the year) instead of $5,000 5 days before year-end:
>
> ECPI percentage = $1.5M pension / ($1.5M pension + $50K accumulation) = 96.8%

> Total income: $260,000 (ordinary income $90K + capital gains $170K)
>
> Taxable income: $260,000 × 3.2% = $8,320
>
> Tax at 15%: $1,248
>
> On the capital gains component alone: $170,000 × 3.2% × 15% = $816
>
> These numbers are still modest. But with larger accumulation amounts, or earlier timing, the impact becomes substantial. The principle is: segregated method requires absolute purity. One dollar breaks it.

Method Two: The Unsegregated Asset Method

The unsegregated method applies when the fund has both pension and accumulation accounts — when some members are in pension phase and others are still accumulating, or when a member has both pension and accumulation accounts simultaneously. Under this method, an actuary certifies the proportion of the fund's assets that are supporting pension liabilities. Investment income and capital gains are then exempt in proportion to that certified percentage.

This method is more flexible but more complex. It requires an actuarial certificate each year. It does not provide the complete capital gains disregard of the segregated method — instead, capital gains are exempt only in proportion to the ECPI percentage. And it requires careful management of the accumulation-to-pension ratio to maximise the exempt percentage.

The practical consequence: trustees who plan to continue making contributions (even modest ones) after commencing a pension should use the unsegregated method and plan their strategy around it from the beginning.

Steve's Four-Day Timing Error: A $45,000 Capital Gains Catastrophe

The ECPI rules create timing risk that many SMSF trustees are unaware of. Steve Morrison's case illustrates this risk with painful precision.

Steve had decided to sell his SMSF's most valuable asset — a commercial property in North Sydney — in June 2023. He had planned to use the pension phase capital gains exemption: the property had appreciated by $300,000 since purchase, and the capital gains tax on $300,000 in pension phase was zero.

His accountant confirmed: 'The sale needs to settle before 30 June. That means contracts need to be signed by mid-June at the latest, given normal settlement timeframes.'

Steve signed contracts on 27 June. The expected settlement date: 30 June.

Settlement occurred on 4 July — 4 days after year-end, due to a delay at the bank.

Under ECPI rules, capital gains are exempt when the disposal occurs in a year when the fund is in full pension phase. The relevant year is the financial year in which settlement occurs. Settlement on 4 July means the gain was realised in the 2023-24 financial year — 1 year later than intended. In 2023-24, Steve's sister had joined the fund as a member still in accumulation phase. The fund was no longer 100% pension phase. The unsegregated method applied, with a pension percentage of 70%.

Capital gain: $300,000. ECPI percentage: 70%. Taxable gain: $90,000. CGT rate (with 15% super tax on taxable capital gains): $90,000 × 10% = $9,000 in additional CGT alone. Including the impact on the fund's ordinary income under the unsegregated ECPI method, total additional tax was approximately $27,000.

Additional consequences: the property had been sold in a year when the market was slightly softer. If Steve had waited until July to settle properly — four more days — the property market might have moved further against him. But the tax planning advice was clear, and the client's instructions were clear: the bank's delay was the variable that Steve could not have controlled.

Steve's avoidable tax cost: approximately $45,000 (including advisor fees, amended assessments, and the tax difference). A four-day bank processing delay. $45,000.

> **$45,000 Steve's timing error — settlement 4 days late**
>
> Planned outcome: $0 CGT in full pension phase. Actual outcome: $90,000 taxable gain due to settlement falling in wrong financial year. Additional tax: approximately $27,000. Restructuring and remediation costs: approximately $18,000. Total: $45,000. Cause: bank settlement delay. Prevention: build a 2-week buffer into all major asset disposals near financial year-end.

NALI and NALE: The Non-Arm's Length Provisions

The NALI (Non-Arm's Length Income) and NALE (Non-Arm's Length Expenses) provisions are among the most aggressive anti-avoidance provisions in the tax law. Their stated purpose: to prevent SMSF members from engineering artificially high income or artificially low expenses through related-party transactions, thereby gaining an unfair advantage from the superannuation tax concessions.

The 2019 amendments to the NALI provisions dramatically expanded their scope and, critically, made them permanent at the asset level. Before 2019, a NALI contamination could often be remediated by restructuring the transaction. After 2019, a contaminated asset remains contaminated for the life of the asset's ownership in the SMSF — regardless of subsequent remediation.

The Three Pathways to 45% Hell

NALI arises through three primary mechanisms:

Pathway One: Below-Market Income

The most common form: the SMSF receives income from a related party at rates below what an arm's-length transaction would produce. Jennifer's rent concession is the archetype. But the definition of 'income' is broad — it includes rent, interest, dividends from related entities, and service fees.

The test is not whether the income is below market. It is whether the terms of the arrangement are different from what would be expected in an arm's-length transaction. A related-party arrangement that replicates exactly what an arm's-length party would provide — same rates, same terms, same conditions, same security — is not NALI, even if the counterparty is a related party.

The practical challenge: demonstrating arm's-length terms when the counterparty is your own family member or company requires contemporaneous documentation. A hastily prepared retrospective comparison is much less persuasive than a market rate analysis conducted before the arrangement was entered into.

Pathway Two: Below-Market Expenses

NALE is the mirror image of NALI: the SMSF incurs expenses at rates below the arm's-length price. If a member provides services to the SMSF for free (or at a discount), or if a related-party adviser charges the SMSF below-market fees, the undercharged amount is treated as NALE — non-arm's length expenditure — and the resulting investment income is contaminated.

This pathway catches many trustees who try to reduce costs by self-managing without professional support. If a trustee performs investment research, property management, or administrative work for the SMSF without charging a market-rate fee, the ATO may characterise the resulting investment income as NALE-contaminated.

Pathway Three: Non-Arm's Length Transactions Creating Future Income

The third and most insidious pathway: a non-arm's length transaction at the acquisition stage that creates future income streams. If an SMSF purchases an asset from a related party at below-market value — paying $400,000 for an asset worth $600,000 — the $200,000 discount means the asset was acquired at artificially favourable terms. All future income from that asset is NALI-contaminated.

This pathway is catching many trustees who believed that acquiring assets at below-market prices from family members was a beneficial strategy. It is not. Every dollar of income earned on an asset that was acquired on non-arm's length terms is taxed at 45% — potentially forever.

Karen's $720,000 Lesson: The NALI Cascade

Karen was 58, a small business owner with an SMSF balance of $1,600,000. In 2020, she decided to restructure her property holdings to take advantage of the pension phase zero-tax concession. She transferred three commercial properties from her personal name into her SMSF.

The 3 properties had market values of approximately $400,000, $350,000, and $500,000. Karen transferred them for $280,000, $250,000, and $350,000 respectively — discounts of 30% in each case. Her reasoning: she was saving stamp duty and CGT by undervaluing them. The ATO wouldn't know — there were no independent valuations.

The ATO did know. Property stamp duty records are public. The ATO's data-matching system identified the discrepancy between Karen's transfer prices and market values within 18 months.

The determination: all 3 properties were acquired on non-arm's length terms. All income from all 3 properties — rent, capital gains on any future sale — was permanently NALI-contaminated. All contaminated income would be taxed at 45%.

Karen's annual rental income from the 3 properties: approximately $120,000. Tax at 45% instead of zero: $54,000 per year. Over the 12 years between 2020 and Karen's expected retirement in 2032: $648,000 in excess tax.

On eventual sale: 3 properties with combined current value of approximately $1.5 million, original SMSF acquisition price $880,000. Capital gain: $620,000. Tax at 45%: $279,000. Tax at pension-phase zero (if no NALI): zero.

Total NALI cost: $648,000 in excess annual taxation plus $279,000 in eventual CGT — approximately $927,000 over the period.

Karen's solicitor pursued the ATO's determination. The outcome was a negotiated settlement in which the ATO agreed to apply the NALI contamination prospectively only, reducing the total liability to approximately $720,000 — still more than the stamp duty and CGT savings that the undervaluation was designed to produce.

> **$720,000 Karen's NALI cascade — cost of below-market property transfers**
>
> Annual excess NALI tax (vs pension phase zero): $54,000/year × estimated 12 years = $648,000. Capital gains NALI tax on eventual sale: $279,000 (estimated). Total before settlement: $927,000. ATO settlement: $720,000. Original saving targeted: stamp duty and CGT estimated at $120,000-$140,000. Net cost: approximately $580,000 more than the cost of doing it properly.

Five Core Principles of SMSF Taxation

The cases in this chapter — Jennifer's $191,250 NALI trap, Steve's $45,000 timing error, Karen's $720,000 cascade — establish 5 principles that every SMSF trustee should understand completely.

Principle One: Pension Phase Is the Destination, Not the Bonus

The 15% accumulation phase tax rate feels advantageous because it is — compared to personal marginal rates of 47%. But accumulation phase is a means to an end, not the end. The goal is pension phase: 0% on all investment income, and complete disregard of capital gains. Planning toward pension phase from the day the fund is established — maintaining an investment strategy that maximises the tax-free income in retirement — is the most important long-term tax planning decision an SMSF trustee makes.

Principle Two: NALI Is Permanent

Before the 2019 NALI reforms, NALI contamination could often be reversed by correcting the underlying transaction. After 2019, it cannot. A NALI-contaminated asset remains contaminated for the life of its ownership in the fund, regardless of what happens subsequently. There are no 'do-overs.' This makes it essential to structure related-party transactions correctly from the beginning — not merely adequately.

Principle Three: Timing Is a Tax Decision

In SMSF tax planning, the timing of transactions — particularly asset disposals — is as important as the structure of the transactions themselves. Selling an asset 4 days after year-end instead of 4 days before year-end can mean the difference between zero tax and substantial tax. Every major asset disposal should be planned with an eye to the financial year, the fund's pension/accumulation status at the relevant time, and the settlement timeline.

Principle Four: Arm's Length Is an Ongoing Obligation

The arm's-length requirement applies to every transaction the SMSF enters into, every year. It is not a one-time structural compliance check — it is a continuous standard. A transaction that was arm's length when it was established can become non-arm's length if circumstances change: if a market rent review is not conducted, if a related party becomes more financially stressed and the SMSF adjusts terms informally, or if the nature of the relationship between the fund and the counterparty changes.

Principle Five: Professional Tax Advice Is a Return-Generating Investment

The cases in this chapter illustrate an important truth: SMSF tax advice is not a cost to be minimised. It is a return-generating investment. Jennifer's $191,250 NALI liability arose because she made a tax-affecting decision (rent pricing) without taking proper tax advice. Karen's $720,000 liability arose because she structured a major transaction without proper tax advice. The cost of that advice — $5,000 to $20,000 for a major transaction review — is invariably lower than the cost of getting the decision wrong.

The SMSF Tax Planning Annual Checklist

Before 30 June each year, review the following with your accountant:

✓ Are all members' pension/accumulation statuses correct and documented?

✓ Are all related-party transactions (rent, loans, services) at independently verified market rates?

✓ Is the investment strategy current and consistent with the actual portfolio?

✓ Are any planned asset disposals timed to fall in the most tax-efficient financial year?

✓ Have all contribution caps been respected, and has any excess been addressed?

✓ Is the ECPI method (segregated vs unsegregated) appropriate for the fund's current member profile?

✓ Are there any transactions from the past year that may have NALI implications?

Chapter Five Summary

The SMSF tax architecture is the fund's most powerful wealth-building feature and its most dangerous liability. The same system that allows a fully retired investor to receive $120,000 per year in rental income, dividends, and capital gains completely tax-free can impose 45% tax on every dollar of income — permanently, at the asset level — if a single related-party transaction is structured incorrectly.

The gap between $0 tax and 45% tax is the largest tax differential available in the Australian tax system. For SMSF members, it is available on both sides: the zero-tax haven is accessible, and the 45% penalty hell is equally accessible. Professional guidance in this area is not optional.

Key Decision	Get It Right	Get It Wrong
Pension phase timing	Zero tax on all income and gains	15% continuing accumulation tax
ECPI method selection	Maximum tax-free income	Partial exemption; actuary required
Related-party transactions	Clean, tax-free income	Permanent 45% NALI contamination
Year-end timing of disposals	Zero CGT in pension phase	$45,000+ in avoidable tax (Steve)
Asset acquisition pricing	Clean investment history	Permanent NALI on all future income

In Chapter Six, we turn from the tax that takes money away from the fund to the insurance that protects what is already there — and the devastating consequences when that protection is absent.

Franking Credits: The Hidden Multiplier in Australian Equity Portfolios

Of all the tax advantages available inside an Australian SMSF, franking credits are perhaps the least understood and most systematically underutilised. This is not because they are obscure — they are one of the signature features of the Australian tax system, and most investors who hold Australian shares are aware of them in the abstract. It is because the specific mechanics of maximising franking credit refunds inside a superannuation fund require both an understanding of the credit system and an active portfolio management approach that many trustees do not maintain.

A franking credit represents the corporate tax already paid on a dividend. Australian companies pay a 30% corporate tax rate on their profits. When those profits are distributed as dividends to shareholders, the dividends come attached to a 'franking credit' equal to the corporate tax already paid. The shareholder can use that credit to offset their personal tax liability.

Inside an SMSF in accumulation phase, the fund's tax rate is 15%. A fully franked dividend carries a franking credit of approximately 43 cents for every dollar of dividend income (reflecting the 30% corporate tax rate). The fund's tax liability on that dollar of dividend income is 15 cents. After applying the forty-three-cent franking credit, the fund not only pays zero tax on the dividend — it receives a refund of ten-eight cents. This is not a rounding error or an accounting technicality. On a large Australian equity portfolio, the franking credit refund can represent a substantial annual cash return.

The Pension Phase Franking Credit Advantage

In pension phase, the ECPI exemption means that the fund pays zero tax on income and capital gains. The 15% tax rate that drives the accumulation phase refund calculation falls to zero. As a result, the entire franking credit on a fully franked dividend becomes refundable. Every single cent of the corporate tax attached to the dividend comes back to the fund.

For a pension-phase SMSF holding $800,000 in Australian shares with an average fully franked dividend yield of 4%, the annual dividend income would be approximately $32,000. The franking credits attached to those dividends, at a full imputation rate, would be approximately $13,700. Every dollar of those credits — which represents tax already paid by the corporate entities that distributed the dividends — is refundable to the pension-phase fund. The after-tax return on that equity portfolio, inclusive of the franking credit refunds, is substantially higher than the headline yield suggests.

Phase	Tax Rate on Income	Franking Credit Treatment	Effective After-Tax Yield (on 4% fully franked dividend)
Personal (marginal 45%)	45%	Reduces tax liability; no refund above tax owed	Approximately 2.9% after tax
Company structure (30%)	30%	Offsets tax; no refund	4.0% after tax (full offset only)
SMSF Accumulation (15%)	15%	Full refund of excess credits	Approximately 5.3% effective yield
SMSF Pension (0%)	0%	Full refund of all credits	Approximately 5.7% effective yield

The comparison is stark. The same investment, held in different tax environments, produces materially different after-tax returns. The pension-phase SMSF advantage is not marginal — it is the difference between a 2.9% after-tax yield and a 5.7% effective yield on the same underlying asset. Multiplied over a ten-year retirement, this difference is transformative.

The Timing Trap: Record Date vs Ex-Dividend Date

To receive a dividend and its associated franking credits, an investor must hold the shares on the 'record date' — the date on which the company determines the list of eligible shareholders. The 'ex-dividend date' is the day the share starts trading without the right to the upcoming dividend, and it typically falls two business days before the record date due to settlement timing.

SMSF trustees who actively manage their equity portfolios — buying and selling individual shares — must be acutely aware of these dates. Selling shares on or after the ex-dividend date but before the record date will result in missing the dividend and the franking credits. Buying shares on the day before the ex-dividend date specifically to capture a dividend (a practice known as 'dividend stripping') was historically employed aggressively by institutional investors and has been subject to increasingly strict ATO scrutiny under Part IVA anti-avoidance provisions.

The practical implication for SMSF trustees: plan significant equity portfolio changes — particularly sales — outside the dividend season unless you have a compelling investment reason to transact. The approximately 3-week period around major dividend distributions (typically August-September and February-March for most ASX companies) is not an optimal time to be selling dividend-paying shares without careful consideration of the franking credit timing.

Capital Gains Tax: The Year-End Calendar That Changes Your Tax Bill

The 15% CGT rate in the accumulation phase of an SMSF, reducible to 10% for assets held more than 12 months, is one of the most powerful tax advantages in the system. But its value is not automatic — it requires active management of when gains are realised and how they are sequenced against available losses.

The Twelve-Month Rule: Not Always as Simple as It Appears

The CGT discount for assets held more than 12 months is a fundamental feature of Australian tax law. Inside an SMSF, a third of the tax is forgiven rather than a half (the personal investor's discount is 50%; the SMSF accumulation phase discount produces an effective rate of 10% rather than 15%). The rule seems simple: hold for 12 months, pay 10%; hold for less than 12 months, pay 15%.

In practice, the calculation is more complex when SMSF assets include multiple parcels of shares or units purchased at different times. When you sell shares in a company that you have been accumulating over 5 years, you must apply a cost base and holding period calculation to each parcel — generally using the FIFO (first in, first out) method as the default, though other methods are available. The result can differ by several thousand dollars depending on which parcels are treated as sold. Your accountant or tax agent should be making these calculations — but you should understand the principle well enough to ask whether the optimal lot identification method has been applied.

Loss Harvesting: Managing Capital Losses Strategically

Capital losses realised inside an SMSF can only be offset against capital gains — they cannot be offset against ordinary income. This means that managing the timing of loss realisation relative to gain realisation is an important annual discipline. Losses that are realised in a year with no corresponding gains are carried forward to future years, where they can be applied when gains are eventually made.

The strategic discipline of loss harvesting — deliberately realising unrealised losses in years where you have significant capital gains — can meaningfully reduce the fund's annual CGT liability. This is not exotic tax planning. It is basic portfolio hygiene that many SMSF trustees fail to practise simply because they are not thinking about their tax position until the financial year is over and the gains are already locked in.

The year-end review meeting in April — which I recommend to all clients — should include a specific review of the fund's unrealised gain and loss position. Positions with significant unrealised losses, particularly those that you may exit in the next 12 months anyway, are candidates for early realisation before June 30. Positions with significant unrealised gains, which you are not planning to exit, benefit from deferral — particularly if the fund is transitioning to pension phase, in which case gains realised after the pension commences are entirely exempt.

Chapter Six

The Insurance Blind Spot

Three professionals. Three different decisions. Three radically different outcomes when disaster arrives.

Picture three 40-year-old professionals in Sydney. All three have SMSFs. All three have accumulated approximately $850,000 in retirement savings. All three consider themselves financially responsible — they have wills, income protection policies, and mortgages they have been diligently repaying.

In 2025, all three are hit by events they did not plan for.

James is struck by a car and sustains spinal injuries that leave him permanently unable to work as a surgeon. Robert dies suddenly of a cardiac arrest, leaving a widow and a $1.45 million SMSF loan still outstanding. Emma's investment property suffers a workplace accident that results in a $1.8 million legal judgment against her SMSF.

Their financial outcomes diverge dramatically — not based on the severity of what happened to them, but based on whether they had structured the right insurance inside their SMSF before it happened.

This is the chapter most SMSF trustees underestimate. In my experience, more retirement security is destroyed by inadequate insurance than by investment violations, tax non-compliance, and estate planning errors combined. The losses do not appear in an ATO penalty notice. They appear slowly, over years, as a fund that should have lasted a lifetime runs dry.

James: The Surgeon Without TPD Insurance

James was 42 years old, a specialist orthopaedic surgeon in Sydney's northern suburbs. His annual income: $480,000. His SMSF balance: $850,000. His mortgage: $900,000. His two children: eight and ten, enrolled in private school at a combined cost of $100,000 per year.

James was disciplined and careful about most financial matters. He had $1 million in life insurance — sufficient, he reasoned, to protect his family if he died. He had income protection insurance paying 75% of salary for 2 years.

He had no TPD (Total and Permanent Disability) insurance.

His reasoning: 'I am a surgeon. I have been trained for 10 years. My hands are steady. I take every precaution.' He had seen TPD policies and found the premiums — approximately $8,000 per year for $1 million of coverage at his age — uncomfortably expensive. He had declined to purchase the cover 5 years earlier and had not revisited the decision.

In March 2025, James was cycling to work when he was struck by a delivery vehicle. The accident caused severe spinal injuries, including partial paralysis of both legs. After 6 months of intensive rehabilitation, James's neurosurgeon delivered the news that James had been refusing to fully accept: he would never return to surgery.

The immediate financial picture: income protection insurance, paying $360,000 annually (75% of $480,000), would continue for 2 years. Beyond that — nothing.

The Mathematics of Long-Term Disability

2 years after the accident, James's income protection benefits expired. The family's expenses had been restructured but remained substantial: mortgage repayments of $55,000 per year; children's school fees of $100,000 per year; living expenses at a reduced but still comfortable $120,000 per year. Total annual requirements: $275,000.

James's SMSF provided some income through pension phase drawdowns — his adviser had commenced a pension under conditional release from the fund to meet the immediate income need

— but the fund balance was being depleted faster than it was growing.

Year	SMSF Balance	Annual Return (7%)	Annual Withdrawal	Remaining
2025 (accident)	$850,000	$59,500	$90,000	$819,500
2026	$819,500	$57,365	$105,000	$771,865
2027 (IP expires)	$771,865	$54,030	$180,000	$645,895
2028	$645,895	$45,213	$180,000	$511,108
2029	$511,108	$35,777	$180,000	$366,885
2030	$366,885	$25,682	$180,000	$212,567
2031	$212,567	$14,880	$180,000	$47,447
2032 (SMSF exhausted)	$47,447	$3,321	$50,767	$0

James's SMSF, which should have sustained him for 30 years of retirement, was exhausted in 7 years. The mortgage — $900,000 — could not be serviced from residual income. In 2032, the family sold their home. The children were removed from private school. James's wife suffered a mental health crisis that required hospitalisation.

> **The Alternative: $1 Million TPD Insurance**
>
> If James had purchased $1 million in TPD (any occupation) insurance at the time of the accident:
>
> TPD payout (2025): $1,000,000.
>
> Revised SMSF total: $1,850,000 ($850K + $1M insurance).

> Annual income at 7%: $129,500.
>
> This fully covers the family's post-accident expenses of $225,000 when combined with James's spouse's income of $95,000.
>
> Mortgage retained. Private school continues. Retirement fund intact.
>
> Annual premium James declined to pay: $8,000.
>
> James, from his wheelchair: 'I declined $8,000 per year in premiums. In return, I lost my house, my children's education, and my wife's health. If I could return to that decision, I would pay one hundred times the premium without a second thought.'

Understanding TPD Insurance: The Critical Distinction

Total and Permanent Disability insurance exists in two fundamentally different forms, and the distinction between them can mean the difference between a claim being paid and a claim being denied.

'Any Occupation' TPD vs 'Own Occupation' TPD

'Any occupation' TPD pays when the insured person is permanently unable to work in any occupation for which they are reasonably suited by education, training, or experience. 'Own occupation' TPD pays when the insured person is permanently unable to work in their specific occupation.

For a surgeon like James, the distinction is enormous. If James can no longer perform surgery but could theoretically teach medical students or provide medico-legal consultancy, an 'any occupation' policy might not pay out — he is not permanently unable to work in any occupation for which he is suited; he is permanently unable to practice surgery specifically. An 'own occupation' policy would pay out in this scenario, because he cannot perform his specific occupation.

The SIS Act creates a complication: SMSFs are permitted to hold 'any occupation' TPD policies under the superannuation trust structure. They are explicitly prohibited from holding 'own occupation' TPD policies inside the SMSF, because 'own occupation' TPD does not satisfy the SIS Act's conditions of release — which require permanent incapacity to work in any suitable occupation, not just the specific current occupation.

This means that a surgeon who holds TPD insurance inside their SMSF, and who becomes permanently unable to perform surgery but could perform other medical work, may find that their SMSF TPD policy does not pay out. The solution: hold 'own occupation' TPD insurance outside the SMSF (funded personally, not through the fund), while 'any occupation' TPD is held inside.

	Own Occupation TPD	**Any Occupation TPD**
Definition	Permanent inability to work in your specific job	Permanent inability to work in any suitable role
Payout trigger	Narrower — easier for claimants to qualify	Broader — harder for claimants to qualify
Premium	Higher	Lower
Inside SMSF?	Prohibited by SIS Act	Permitted
Suitable for	Specialists, high-skill professionals	General protection
Recommended for professionals	Hold OUTSIDE SMSF	Hold INSIDE SMSF

David vs Emma: The Occupation Definition in Practice

David and Emma were both physiotherapists at the same practice. Both were 45 years old. Both suffered severe hand injuries in separate incidents in the same year.

David held 'own occupation' TPD insurance outside his SMSF: $1.2 million, premiums $7,200 per year, covering his inability to practice physiotherapy. Emma held 'any occupation' TPD insurance inside her SMSF: $1.2 million, premiums $5,400 per year.

David's injury: irreparable damage to the median nerve in his right hand, making fine manual therapy impossible. He could no longer practice as a physiotherapist. His 'own occupation' policy paid $1.2 million immediately. Total premium outlay over 15 years: $108,000. Net recovery: $1,092,000.

Emma's injury: similar damage to her left hand. She was right-handed. Her insurer assessed her capacity for other occupations: she could theoretically teach physiotherapy, supervise students, or provide rehabilitation consulting. She was not 'unable to work in any occupation for which she was reasonably suited.' Her 'any occupation' claim was denied.

Emma's outcome: no TPD payout. 15 years of premiums ($5,400 × 15 = $81,000) wasted. She eventually retrained as a practice administrator, at a salary reduction of $80,000 per year compared to her clinical work.

> ## $1,200,000 Emma's occupation-definition mismatch
>
> Insurance paid: $0. Total premiums paid: $81,000. Annual income reduction vs physiotherapy: $80,000/year. Ten-year income cost: $800,000. David's outcome with correct insurance: $1.2M payout after $108K in premiums. The $1,800 annual premium difference between own-occupation and any-occupation was the hinge on which $1.2 million turned.

Life Insurance: Getting the Coverage Amount Right

Life insurance inside an SMSF is straightforward in concept: the fund holds a term life policy (and potentially a terminal illness policy), premiums are paid from the fund's assets, and the benefit is paid into the fund on the member's death, forming part of the death benefit distributed to beneficiaries.

The most common mistake with life insurance is underestimating the amount needed. Sarah Thompson's case, while ultimately a success story, illustrates the calculation clearly.

Sarah's $1.5M Life Insurance: Adequate But Not Optimal

Sarah was 40 years old, an accountant with a $500,000 SMSF and a busy two-income household. Her financial adviser ran the numbers for her in 2023:

Liability	Amount	Basis
Mortgage balance	$600,000	Outstanding home loan
Children's schooling (2 children, 11 years)	$400,000	$18,000/year × 2 children × 11 years avg
University education	$200,000	$25,000/year × 2 children × 4 years
Spouse's living costs (to age 67)	$1,620,000	$60,000/year × 27 years
Funeral and estate costs	$20,000	Standard estimate
TOTAL NEEDS	$2,840,000	

Less existing assets (SMSF + savings + home equity)	$1,000,000	
INSURANCE SHORTFALL	$1,840,000	Recommended coverage

The adviser recommended $2 million. Sarah chose $1.5 million, balancing coverage against premium cost.

In 2025, Sarah suffered a cerebral haemorrhage and died at age 42. The $1.5 million insurance payout into the SMSF, combined with the existing $550,000 balance, gave the fund $2,050,000.

Her husband Tom, with professional advisory guidance, structured the fund's assets to repay the mortgage ($600,000), establish an education reserve ($600,000), and maintain a $850,000 income-producing balance. Annual drawdown at 6%: $51,000, supplemented by Tom's salary, provided sufficient family income.

The children completed the school. Tom retained the home. The family's life trajectory, while permanently altered by Sarah's death, was not financially destroyed.

Tom's later reflection: 'Sarah's insurance was not quite enough — we had to make some adjustments. If she had taken the $2 million recommendation, we would have been much more comfortable. But the $1.5 million she chose was enough to protect the most important things.'

Emma's Public Liability Nightmare: Insurance the SMSF Cannot Afford to Skip

Emma's SMSF held a $1.2 million investment property in Bondi, purchased in 2020. Emma had purchased building insurance ($500,000) and contents insurance ($50,000). She had not purchased public liability insurance.

Her reasoning: 'The property has tenants with their own renter's insurance. The building insurance covers structural damage. Why would I need public liability?'

In August 2021, Emma hired a plumber to repair a water leak in the property's roof space. The plumber, while working in the attic, stepped through an area of degraded ceiling material and fell three metres to the floor below. The injury was catastrophic: severe spinal damage resulting in permanent partial paralysis.

The plumber's family filed suit against Emma's SMSF as the property owner, claiming $2.5 million in medical costs, lifetime care, lost income, and general damages. The court found that Emma's SMSF had failed in its duty of care as a property owner — the attic flooring was aged and showed visible signs of stress; a reasonable property owner would have identified and repaired it. The judgment: $1,800,000 (the court assessed the property owner's liability at 70%).

Emma's SMSF had $1.5 million in total assets. The judgment of $1.8 million exceeded the fund's entire net asset base.

$1,800,000 Emma's public liability judgment — SMSF depleted

Court judgment: $1,800,000 (70% liability). SMSF total assets: $1,500,000. Shortfall: $300,000, paid from Emma's personal savings. The SMSF was completely depleted. Emma's retirement plan — retire at 60 with $2M — became: work until 67, build SMSF from zero. Annual public liability premium she declined to pay: $800. Ten-year premium total: $8,000. Emma: 'I saved $8,000. I lost $1.8M and 7 years of retirement.'

What Insurance Can an SMSF Hold?

Insurance Type	SMSF Permitted?	Notes
Life insurance	Yes	Tax-effective; premiums deductible to fund
TPD (any occupation)	Yes	Must be 'any occupation' definition only
TPD (own occupation)	No (inside SMSF)	Must be held outside; does not satisfy SIS Act conditions of release
Income protection	Yes	Permitted inside SMSF; specific payment structure requirements
Critical illness / trauma	No	Does not satisfy conditions of release; must be held outside SMSF
Building / contents	Yes (for owned property)	Standard property insurance; not a release condition issue
Public liability	Yes (for owned property)	Critically important; often overlooked
Collectibles insurance	Yes (mandatory)	Required within 7 days of acquisition under Reg 13.18AA

Income Protection Inside an SMSF: The Key Restriction

Income protection insurance can be held inside an SMSF, but with an important restriction: payments can only commence once the member has completely ceased their usual employment. Ancillary benefits — partial disability benefits, rehabilitation benefits, and return-to-work programs that are common in retail income protection policies — are not permitted inside the SMSF structure, because they do not satisfy the conditions of release.

The practical consequence: for many professionals, it may be better to hold income protection insurance outside the SMSF (funded with after-tax personal income) to access the full range of policy features, while holding life and TPD insurance inside the SMSF to take advantage of the tax deductibility of premiums to the fund.

The Insurance Planning Framework

The correct approach to insurance planning in an SMSF is not to maximise the amount of insurance held inside the structure. It is to match the insurance held inside and outside the structure to the specific financial risks the fund and the member face.

Step One: Quantify the Liabilities

The starting point for insurance planning is a complete picture of the financial liabilities the insurance needs to address: the outstanding mortgage and any other debts; the income needs of dependants if the insured person dies or becomes permanently disabled; the cost of maintaining the household and funding children's education; and any specific obligations that flow from the SMSF's investment structure (such as LRBA loans, as in Robert's case).

Step Two: Map Insurance to Liabilities

Life insurance should be sized to cover the total liability shortfall after accounting for existing assets. TPD insurance should match the liability calculation for life insurance but be held in the appropriate structure (any-occupation inside SMSF; own-occupation outside). LRBA loans require dedicated loan-repayment insurance inside the SMSF. Investment property insurance (building, contents, and public liability) must be maintained at adequate levels for each property.

Step Three: Review Annually

Insurance requirements change as financial circumstances change. A mortgage that is being repaid reduces the life insurance requirement. A new LRBA loan increases the requirement for loan-repayment coverage. Children leaving school reduces the income protection requirement. The annual insurance review — conducted as part of the annual investment strategy review — is where these changes are captured and addressed.

The SMSF Insurance Checklist

Life insurance: Amount covers total liability shortfall after existing assets. Reviewed annually against current liabilities.

TPD (any occupation, inside SMSF): Amount matches the life insurance calculation. Occupation definition confirmed as 'any occupation' — not 'own occupation.'

TPD (own occupation, outside SMSF): For professionals whose specific occupation is their primary income source. Held personally, not through SMSF.

Income protection: Held inside or outside SMSF depending on benefit requirements. Two-year vs five- year vs to-age-65 benefit period reviewed.

LRBA loan insurance: Dedicated coverage equal to outstanding loan balance at each annual review date.

Property insurance: Building, contents, and PUBLIC LIABILITY for every property the SMSF holds. Never skip the public liability.

> Critical illness: Cannot be held inside SMSF. Should be held personally if appropriate to the member's risk profile.

Chapter Six Summary

The insurance chapter is the one that most SMSF trustees read after they should have read it. Insurance decisions are easy to defer — the premium is a certain cost today; the benefit is an uncertain payment at an uncertain future date. The psychological tendency is to undervalue the future protection and overvalue the present premium saving.

James, Robert, and Emma each made that undervaluation. The cost: financial ruin in James's case, acute crisis in Robert's case, and complete SMSF depletion in Emma's case.

The correct framing for SMSF insurance is not 'how much does this cost?' It is 'what is the maximum financial damage that could occur if I am not insured, and how does that compare to the premium?'

For James, the answer was: premiums of $8,000 per year versus a potential loss of everything. He paid the wrong way. For Emma, the answer was: premiums of $800 per year versus a $1.8 million judgment. She paid the wrong way too.

In Chapter Seven, we examine the rules that govern how money moves into and out of an SMSF — and the remarkably specific timing and threshold requirements that catch unprepared trustees with alarming regularity.

The Underinsurance Crisis: Why Australia's Retirement Savers Are Exposed

The superannuation system has contributed to the problem in an unintended way. The automatic insurance provisions that existed in many default superannuation funds — where all members received default life and TPD coverage without actively choosing it — provided a floor of coverage that, while inadequate for most members, was at least something. The 2019 Protecting Your Super package changed this, requiring that insurance be 'opt-in' rather than automatic for members with low balances, young members (under ten-five), and inactive accounts. The intent — protecting members from paying premiums on coverage they did not need or want — produced the unintended consequence of a significant reduction in insurance coverage among the most vulnerable groups.

For SMSF members, insurance is never automatic. It must be actively selected, structured, and implemented. The default is no insurance — and the consequence of no insurance, in the event of serious illness or death, is the exposure of a fund that may represent the entire financial foundation of a family's retirement.

The Four Triggers for Insurance Review

Insurance needs are not static. They change as life circumstances change, and the insurance coverage that was appropriate at1 life stage is frequently inappropriate — too much, too little, or the wrong type — at another. In my practice, I conduct insurance reviews at4 specific triggers: at SMSF establishment; when the member acquires a significant liability (particularly a property LRBA); when there is a significant life event (marriage, divorce, birth of a child, death of a co-member); and every 3 years as a matter of routine.

The most commonly missed trigger is the LRBA acquisition. When an SMSF borrows to purchase a $1.5 million commercial property, the fund has incurred a liability that, in a worst-case scenario (the member's death or disability), may need to be repaid urgently. If the only member of the fund dies, the LRBA does not automatically disappear — the loan remains outstanding, the bank requires repayment according to the loan terms, and the asset may need to be sold in an unfavourable market to meet the obligation. Life insurance structured to cover the LRBA balance eliminates this risk. The absence of that insurance transforms a legitimate investment strategy into a potential crisis for a surviving spouse or family.

Life Stage / Trigger	Insurance Need Change	Action Required
SMSF establishment	Baseline coverage needs assessment	Full insurance needs analysis; implement life, TPD, IP as appropriate
LRBA acquisition	Loan liability creates specific death/disability risk	Increase life and TPD to cover at minimum the LRBA balance outstanding
Major income increase	Replacement income need increases	Review income protection benefit levels; increase if needed
Marriage / de facto relationship	Dependent now exists; estate planning implications	Review life insurance quantum; update BDBN to include partner
Birth of child	Financial dependant; education cost exposure	Increase life insurance; consider child trauma cover
Children become financially independent	Dependency exposure reduces	Review whether life insurance quantum is still appropriate; may be able to reduce
Mortgage paid off	Liability reduced	Review whether life insurance

		quantum can be reduced
Retirement / pension phase	Income replacement no longer relevant; wealth transfer focus	Review IP (may no longer be needed); review life insurance for estate planning

Income Protection Inside vs Outside Superannuation: The Structural Comparison

Income protection insurance is one of the most valuable forms of personal insurance available to working Australians — but its optimal placement, inside or outside superannuation, involves a set of trade-offs that are frequently misunderstood.

Income protection insurance pays a monthly benefit — typically 75% of pre-disability income — if the insured is unable to work due to illness or injury. The benefit period typically runs for 2 years, 5 years, or to age 65, and a waiting period of thirty, sixty, or 90 days applies before benefits commence.

Feature	Inside Superannuation	Outside Superannuation
Premium funding	Pre-tax dollars (via employer SG or salary sacrifice)	Post-tax dollars
Tax on benefits	Benefits taxed when withdrawn from superannuation	Benefits taxed as income at marginal rate when received
Benefit type available	Indemnity value only	Indemnity value only

Benefit payment timing	Must meet condition of release to access; may delay payment	Benefits paid directly to insured without superannuation gate
Premium deductibility (employed)	Not directly deductible by the member	Deductible by employed workers
Premium deductibility (self-employed)	Funded pre-tax via contributions; effective deductibility	Deductible to self-employed as a business expense
Benefit period limitation	No structural limitation, but SIS Act conditions of release apply	No limitation — benefits paid for the agreed period

The structural case for holding income protection inside superannuation is strongest for members who are not self-employed and whose premiums are funded through salary sacrifice or employer contributions — effectively paying with pre-tax dollars. The tax saving on premiums can be meaningful for high-income earners.

However, the tax advantage of holding income protection inside superannuation is less decisive than it is for life and TPD cover, because income protection premiums paid outside superannuation are tax deductible to the individual regardless of employment status. This means the after-tax cost of premiums is similar whether the policy is held inside or outside superannuation. But for people who have maximised or are close to the concessional contribution cap, holding income protection cover outside super may be more beneficial.

The structural case for holding income protection outside superannuation is strongest for members who want immediate benefit access without the superannuation release-of-benefits gate.

For most SMSF members, normally the optimal approach is to hold income protection outside superannuation — primarily for the access and flexibility advantages — given that the premium tax deductibility available outside superannuation largely neutralises the pre-tax funding benefit available inside.

The Claims Process: What Happens When You Need to Use Your Insurance

Many members give extensive thought to the acquisition of insurance and almost none to the claims process. This is understandable — nobody wants to dwell on the circumstances that would trigger a claim. But the claims process is where the quality of your insurance arrangement is tested, and its complexity is frequently a source of additional distress at an already difficult time.

For life insurance claims in an SMSF: the claimant is the fund, not the individual beneficiary. The insurance proceeds are paid to the fund and then distributed to the beneficiaries according to the death benefit rules — BDBN, trustee discretion, or reversionary pension. The insurer will require the death certificate, proof of policy, fund trustee details, and in some cases a completed claim form. The entire process typically takes four to 8 weeks for straightforward claims, longer for contested or complex cases.

For TPD claims in an SMSF: the same mechanism applies — the insurance proceeds enter the fund and then must be paid to the member as a lump sum or pension, subject to the relevant condition of release (total and permanent disability). The definition of TPD in the policy — which in SMSF must be the 'any occupation' definition — is assessed by the insurer, not by the trustees. If the insurer's assessment differs from the member's expectation, a dispute may arise that requires engagement with the Australian Financial Complaints Authority (AFCA) or the courts.

The most important practical step you can take in relation to insurance claims is this: know where your policies are, know the policy numbers, and ensure that at least one other person in your family knows these details and can access them in an emergency. Insurance that cannot be found is insurance that cannot be claimed.

Business Risk Insurance: The SMSF as a Business Continuity Tool

For SMSF members who are business owners, the SMSF can play a role in the broader business risk management strategy. Specifically, where the SMSF holds the business's operating premises under a business real property LRBA, key person insurance and buy-sell insurance held within the SMSF can provide a mechanism for funding the transfer of business ownership in the event of a key person's death or disability.

The mechanics are complex and require specific legal and accounting advice, but the principle is straightforward: a business owned by 2 partners can use life insurance on each partner's life, held within each partner's SMSF, to fund the buyout of the other partner's business interest in the event of death or disability. The buy-sell agreement is documented in the partnership or shareholder agreement, and the insurance proceeds — once received by the fund and distributed to the deceased's estate — provide the liquidity for the surviving partner to acquire the deceased's share.

This structure, when properly implemented, provides business continuity certainty, eliminates the forced-sale risk of needing to find an external buyer under time pressure, and ensures that the deceased partner's family receives fair value for their interest. It is not suitable for all business types or all partnership arrangements — the specific circumstances must be carefully assessed. But for SMSF members who own professional practices, medical facilities, or other businesses with significant goodwill value, the business continuity insurance structure is worth exploring with a specialist adviser.

Chapter 7

The Contribution Labyrinth

Getting Money In — and Getting It Back Out — Without Destroying What You've Built

There is a particular kind of financial tragedy that does not announce itself with a market crash or an auditor's letter. It arrives quietly, on an ordinary Tuesday, when a well-meaning trustee deposits money into their SMSF 6 days before June 30, assuming it will be processed in time — or withdraws $120,000 from the wrong account — or accepts a block of shares their son transferred as a birthday gift. No alarm sounds. No error message appears. The contribution processes normally. The transfer registers cleanly. And then, months or years later, the Australian Taxation Office arrives with a calculation that politely dismantles the gains of a decade.

I have watched this happen more times than I care to count. And almost every time, the trustee's first words are the same: 'But I didn't know there were rules about that.' They are not foolish people. They are, more often than not, highly educated professionals who applied careful intelligence to their investment strategy while assuming that the administrative mechanics — putting money in, taking money out — were self-explanatory. They were not.

Chapter Seven is about those mechanics. It is the most rule-dense chapter in this book, and deliberately so, because the rules around contributions and withdrawals are numerous, interconnected, and unforgiving of partial knowledge. But rules without context are dry and forgettable. So we will move through the framework by following three people whose very different journeys illuminate why these rules exist — and what happens when they are misunderstood.

The Contributions Landscape: A Structural Overview

Before we enter the stories, it helps to understand the two fundamental categories into which every superannuation contribution falls. The first is concessional contributions — money that goes in before tax has been paid on it, and which is therefore taxed at 15% inside the fund. The second is non-concessional contributions — money that has already been taxed in the member's hands, and which therefore enters the fund without further tax on the way in.

This distinction matters because the rules governing how much can be contributed, when, and by whom are entirely different for each category. Confuse them, and you may find yourself facing excess contributions tax — a penalty that can easily exceed the tax benefit you were hoping to obtain.

Contribution Type	Who Pays Tax	Annual Cap (2025-26)	Source
Concessional (before-tax)	Fund at 15%	$30,000	Employer SG, salary sacrifice, personal deductible
Non-Concessional (after-tax)	Already taxed	$120,000	Personal post-tax contributions
Downsizer	Nil (special category)	$300,000 per person	Proceeds from principal residence sale with conditions
Government Co-Contribution	Nil	Up to $500	Govt matches low-income earner contributions
Spouse Contribution	Nil (up to $540 rebate)	Counts toward	Contribution by spouse on

		recipient's NCC cap	behalf of member

Steven's Story: The 28 Day Rule That Nobody Told Him About

Steven Li had been self-employed for 17 years. He ran a mid-sized civil engineering consultancy in Brisbane, had built his SMSF from $380,000 to a little over $1.1 million, and managed his contributions with what he considered meticulous attention. Every year, shortly before June 30, he would consult his accountant, determine his concessional and non-concessional caps, and make his contributions accordingly. The system worked.

Steven was 69. He understood that the work test — the requirement to work at least 40 hours in any 30 consecutive days — applied to members aged 67 to 74 who wished to claim a tax deduction for their personal contributions. He had read that from 1 July 2022, the work test had been removed entirely for non-concessional contributions: members under 75 could make after-tax contributions without any employment test. He had noted this change with satisfaction. Then, in late June of a year in which business had been particularly strong, he decided to maximise his concessional cap — making a $27,500 personal contribution intending to claim it as a tax deduction for that financial year.

On June 28 he called his bank and instructed the transfer of $27,500 to his SMSF. The money was received by the fund on June 30. Steven felt satisfied. He was maximising his concessional position for the year efficiently and legally, exactly as intended. What he did not know was that it was not the receipt date that mattered — it was the allocation date.

What Steven did not know was that under SIS Regulation 7.08, a trustee must allocate a contribution to a member's account within 28 days after the end of the month in which it is received. And under ATO Tax Determination TD 2013/22, it is the date of allocation — not the date of receipt — that determines which financial year the contribution counts against. His SMSF administrator, processing a backlog of June-end transactions, allocated Steven's contribution to his account on 3 July. Under TD 2013/22, the $27,500 counted against the new financial year's concessional cap — not the year he had intended.

> **The 28 Day Allocation Rule — What It Requires**
>
> Under SIS Reg 7.08, trustees must allocate contributions to a member's account within 28 days after the end of the month in which they are received. Under TD 2013/22, a contribution received in June but allocated in July counts toward the new financial year's cap — not the year of receipt. Always initiate end-of-year contributions no later than 20 June to allow adequate processing time. Note: as of 1 July 2022, the work test no longer applies to non-concessional contributions for members under 75. The work test (40 hours in any 30 consecutive days) continues to apply only where a member aged 67–74 wishes to claim a tax deduction for a personal contribution.

Steven's accountant filed that year's return claiming a deduction for $27,500. The ATO cross-matched this against the SMSF annual return, which reported the contribution as allocated in July. The mismatch was flagged immediately. An audit was initiated. Meanwhile, in August of the new financial year, Steven had made a second personal deductible contribution of $27,500 — not realising the June contribution was already counting against the new year's $30,000 cap. He was now $25,000 over the concessional cap for the new financial year.

The $25,000 excess concessional contribution was included in Steven's assessable income for the new financial year and taxed at his marginal rate of 47%, less a 15% tax offset for contributions tax already paid by the fund. The net additional tax: approximately $8,000. Amended returns, audit fees, and professional costs to resolve the breach added another $23,000. Total preventable loss:

approximately $31,000 — caused entirely by a two-day gap between when a contribution was instructed and when it was processed.

> **$31,000 Steven's Preventable Audit Cost**
>
> A contribution received on 30 June but allocated on 3 July shifted $27,500 into the new financial year's concessional cap. A second $27,500 contribution in August created a $25,000 excess. Net additional tax plus professional remediation costs: $31,000.

The lesson is not that the allocation rule is obscure or unreasonable. It is that contribution timing decisions made in the final days of June carry risks that are invisible to the uninitiated. Steven's administrator was following standard practice; his accountant had assumed the contribution would count in the year it was instructed. Neither had modelled the gap between receipt and allocation. A June 20 transfer date would have eliminated the risk entirely.

I now advise every client to initiate end-of-financial-year contributions no later than June 20 — not June 28. Bank settlement, administrative processing, and public holidays can all create gaps between an instruction and an allocation. For members aged 67 to 74 who intend to claim a tax deduction for personal contributions, the work test requirement (40 hours in any thirty consecutive days during the financial year) remains essential to document, as it continues to apply to deductible contributions — though, importantly, the work test no longer applies to non-concessional contributions for anyone under seventy-five.

The Bring-Forward Rule: A Powerful Tool, Precisely Bounded

The bring-forward rule allows eligible members — those under 75 at the beginning of a financial year — to contribute up to 3 times the annual non-concessional cap in a single year, or over a rolling three-year period. At the 2025-26 cap of $120,000 per year, this means a potential single contribution of $360,000 (or a staged contribution totalling $360,000 over 3 years), subject to the member's Total Superannuation Balance not exceeding the relevant threshold.

The three-year period, once triggered, is irrevocable. If you contribute $360,000 in year one, you have exhausted your non-concessional cap for the following two financial years. Any further personal contribution in years two or three will be an excess non-concessional contribution. Many trustees understand this in the abstract but fail to plan for the practical implications when unexpected income arrives.

TSB at June 30 Prior Year	Bring-Forward Available	Maximum 3-Year Contribution
Under $1.76M (2025-26)	Full bring-forward	$360,000
$1.76M – $1.88M	Two-year bring-forward	$240,000
$1.88M – $2M	1 year only (no bring-forward)	$120,000
At or above $2M	No non-concessional contributions permitted	$0

The bring-forward thresholds change with indexation. What was accurate when I first drafted this chapter may shift by the time you read it. Always verify current thresholds before making a large contribution. This is not a disclaimer offered out of professional caution — it is a statement about the genuine pace of regulatory change in this area.

Emily's Story: The In-Specie Contribution That Became a Tax Event

Emily was a 54-year-old radiologist who had spent the better part of her career accumulating a portfolio of high-quality listed shares — BHP, CSL, Westpac, Macquarie — outside of superannuation. When she established her SMSF in late 2021, her financial planner suggested that instead of selling the shares and contributing cash, she simply transfer them directly into the SMSF as an in-specie contribution. The assets would remain unchanged; only the legal ownership would shift. It seemed elegant. It seemed efficient.

What Emily's planner did not fully explain — or what Emily did not fully absorb in the midst of a complex transaction — was that an in-specie contribution of non-cash assets triggers CGT as if those assets had been sold at market value on the date of transfer. The SMSF was acquiring assets from a related party. Even though Emily was transferring her own shares, the legislation treats the transfer as a deemed disposal.

> **In-specie Contributions — The CGT Trigger**
>
> When a member transfers assets into their SMSF as a non-concessional contribution, CGT applies as if the assets were sold at market value on the transfer date. This applies even if the member personally owned the assets before the transfer. The contribution value is the market value of the assets on the day of transfer.

Emily's shares had a cost base of $340,000. Their market value at the time of transfer was $610,000. The deemed capital gain was $270,000. Emily had held the shares for over 12 months, so she was entitled to the 50% CGT discount — but that still left a $135,000 taxable capital gain, assessed at her marginal rate of 45%. The additional tax payable: $60,750.

The shares themselves went into the SMSF at their market value cost base of $610,000. Future gains within the fund would be taxed at 15% (or zero in pension phase). The long-term outcome was still favourable — Emily ultimately came out ahead because of the substantial tax advantage inside superannuation. But she had not budgeted for the immediate $60,750 tax bill on income she had not actually received. It was, as she put it to me, 'the most expensive lesson I've ever had about the word deemed.'

The alternative — and the approach I now recommend as a first consideration for similar situations — is to sell the shares outside superannuation, contribute the proceeds as a cash non-concessional contribution, and let the SMSF purchase the same or equivalent shares. Yes, you still pay CGT on the capital gain from the sale. But you have control over the timing, you can plan around tax-loss harvesting opportunities, and you avoid the administrative complexity of an in-specie transfer valuation. The CGT event is identical either way — but the planning options are substantially better.

> **$60,750 Emily's In-specie Transfer Tax Surprise**
>
> Deemed disposal CGT on $270,000 gain from in-specie share transfer to SMSF, at 45% marginal rate with 50% CGT discount. An unbudgeted tax bill on income never actually received.

What Assets Can Be Transferred In-specie?

The general rule is that SMSFs cannot acquire assets from related parties — and members are related parties. However, there are specific exceptions, and understanding them is essential for any trustee with significant assets outside superannuation.

Asset Type	In-specie Transfer to SMSF	Conditions
Listed securities (shares, ETFs, bonds)	Permitted	Must be at market value; CGT applies as deemed disposal

Business real property	Permitted	Must be used wholly and exclusively in business; market value required
Unlisted unit trusts (widely held)	Permitted with conditions	Must meet specific definition; complex analysis required
Residential property	Prohibited	Cannot be acquired from a related party under any circumstances
Collectibles (art, cars, wine)	Prohibited	Cannot be acquired from a related party
Unlisted shares in private companies	Generally prohibited	Exception only for certain widely held vehicles

The prohibition on residential property bears emphasis. I have spoken to dozens of members who assumed they could transfer their investment property — or even a holiday house — into their SMSF to shelter the rental income and eventual capital gain. They cannot. Residential property simply cannot be acquired from a related party. Full stop. No valuation, no market rate, no legal structuring workaround exists. If you want residential property in your SMSF, the fund must purchase it from an unrelated vendor on the open market.

The Transfer Balance Cap: The Boundary on Tax-Free Retirement Income

If the contribution rules govern how money enters superannuation, the Transfer Balance Cap governs the gateway to tax-free retirement income. It is, in my view, the single most important piece of superannuation reform of the past decade — and one of the most misunderstood.

From July 1, 2017, the government introduced a lifetime cap on the total superannuation benefits that could be transferred into the tax-free retirement phase. Initially set at $1.6 million, this cap has been indexed and, from 1 July 2025, stands at $2 million per person. The principle is straightforward: you can shelter up to $2 million inside a tax-free pension, but beyond that threshold, the tax advantages of the pension phase do not apply.

The practical implications, however, are anything but straightforward. And the story of Richard and Margaret Hartley illustrates why.

Richard and Margaret: The $190,000 Sequencing Error

Richard Hartley was 63, Margaret 61. Together, they had built an SMSF with approximately $4.2 million — Richard's balance approximately $2.4 million, Margaret's approximately $2 million. When Richard turned 65 and decided to commence an account-based pension, his financial planner advised him to transfer his entire $2.4 million into pension phase.

The error was elementary but catastrophic. Richard's Transfer Balance Cap was $2 million. He transferred $2.4 million. The excess was $400,000. The ATO assessed an excess transfer balance amount and charged earnings tax on the notional earnings of the excess during the period it remained in the pension account. Because the error was not detected for 11 months — it was identified only at the annual audit — those earnings had accumulated substantially.

The total excess transfer balance tax paid: approximately $47,000. Richard was required to commute $400,000 back from pension phase into accumulation phase, paying 15% tax on future earnings from that portion. The long-term forward cost — accumulated over the remaining years of his retirement — was estimated at an additional $143,000 in tax relative to have the transfer been structured correctly.

> **$190,000 Richard's Transfer Balance Excess — Lifetime Cost**

> $47,000 immediate excess transfer balance tax + estimated $143,000 additional tax over retirement compared to correct structuring of a $2M pension transfer.

The solution, had the plan been structured correctly, was almost embarrassingly simple. Transfer $2 million into pension phase. Leave $400,000 in accumulation. The accumulation balance of $400,000 would pay 15% tax on earnings — not zero, but a far cry from the alternative. Meanwhile, Margaret's $2 million was perfectly positioned to utilise her full Transfer Balance Cap. Together, the couple could shelter $4 million in tax-free pension phase — a significant and entirely achievable outcome.

> **The Transfer Balance Cap — Key Rules**
>
> Each person has a personal Transfer Balance Cap (currently $2M for 2025-26 onwards, subject to future indexation). This is a lifetime cap — once you use it, any subsequent commencement of additional retirement phase income streams counts against it. If you exceed the cap, the ATO assesses an 'excess transfer balance tax' on notional earnings of the excess. Your personal cap may be less than $2M if you began a pension before 1 July 2025 (proportional indexation applies).

Minimum Pension Requirements: The Annual Non-Negotiable

Once money is in retirement phase — once the pension has commenced — the law imposes a minimum annual payment requirement. This is not optional. It is not discretionary. And failing to meet it carries consequences that cannot be easily reversed.

The minimum pension percentage is calculated on the account balance at the start of each financial year (or at the commencement of the pension for the first year) and varies by age.

Age of Pensioner	Minimum Annual Drawdown	On a $2M Balance
Under 65	4%	$80,000
65–74	5%	$100,000
75–79	6%	$120,000
80–84	7%	$140,000
85–89	9%	$180,000
90–94	11%	$220,000
95+	14%	$280,000

If a trustee fails to make the minimum pension payment in a given financial year, the ATO deems the pension to have never commenced for that year. The fund loses the tax exemption on pension assets — the ECPI exemption — for that entire year. All income and gains that would have been tax-free become taxable at 15%. For a large pension fund, this can represent a six-figure tax bill for a single administrative oversight.

The June Trap

Every year, without fail, I receive calls in July from trustees who have not yet paid their minimum pension by 30 June. Some have invested all available cash. Some have simply forgotten. Some assumed they could 'top it up' in the final weeks of the year. The calls are stressful. The solutions are expensive.

The structural risk here is concentration in illiquid assets. A trustee who holds 90% of their SMSF in direct property and 10%in a term deposit that has not yet matured faces a genuine liquidity problem. The minimum pension must be paid from accessible funds. If those funds are not available — if you cannot make the payment without breaking a term deposit or selling an asset — you face a choice between a penalty (breaking the deposit) and a potentially much larger penalty (losing ECPI for the year).

My standing recommendation: maintain a cash or liquid ETF component of your SMSF sufficient to cover at least 18 months of minimum pension payments. This is not dead money. It is insurance against the illiquidity traps that property-heavy portfolios create. The cost of carrying slightly more cash than strictly necessary is trivially small compared to the cost of a single lost ECPI year.

The Withdrawal Framework: Conditions of Release

Just as the contribution rules determine how money gets into superannuation, the 'conditions of release' framework determines when and how it can come out. Superannuation is a long-term savings vehicle protected by preservation rules — most members cannot access their benefits until they satisfy a condition of release.

Condition of Release	Minimum Age	Access Type	Key Notes
Reaching preservation age and retiring	60	Full unrestricted access	Must have ceased employment arrangement
Reaching age 65	65	Full unrestricted access	No employment test required
Transition to Retirement (TTR)	60 (preservation age)	Pension only, 4%-10% max per year	Cannot receive lump sum; limited to 4%-10% of opening balance

Permanent incapacity	Any age	Full access	Medical certification required; complex definitions apply
Terminal illness	Any age	Full tax-free access	Two independent medical certifications required
Severe financial hardship	55+ (with 26 weeks unemployment) or any age (extreme)	Limited lump sum ($10K–$10K range)	Limited amounts; strict criteria
Death	N/A	Death benefit payment	Complex rules re: dependants, tax treatment, binding nominations

The Proportional Rule: Tax-Free vs Taxable Components

Here is a rule that catches even experienced trustees off guard: when you withdraw a benefit from superannuation, you cannot choose to take only from the tax-free component or only from the taxable component. The proportional rule requires that every withdrawal contain the same ratio of tax-free to taxable components as the overall account balance.

Why does this matter? Because the taxable component (especially the taxed element) can be taxed differently depending on your age and whether you take the benefit as a lump sum or an income stream. For people who have reached preservation age but are under 60, taxable components of pension payments are generally taxed at marginal rates, usually with a 15% tax offset on the taxed element.

For lump sums paid to someone who has reached preservation age but is under 60, concessional treatment can apply up to the low-rate cap (which is $260,000 for 2025–26, lifetime), with tax applying above that cap under the relevant rules.

From age 60, super benefits from a taxed fund are commonly tax-free (both pension payments and lump sums, subject to the usual conditions).

The proportional rule becomes especially significant in death benefits, a topic we will explore in depth in Chapter Eight. For now, the key takeaway is that accumulating a larger tax-free component (often built via non-concessional contributions) can reduce tax outcomes where benefits are paid to non-dependant beneficiaries, because tax-free amounts remain tax-free while taxable components may be taxed.

Marcus and Linda: Building the Tax-Free Component Deliberately

Marcus was 58 and planning to retire at 62. His SMSF had $1.4 million — $940,000 taxable component, $460,000 tax-free component (roughly 33% tax-free). His adult daughter Jennifer was not a dependant for superannuation purposes.

Marcus's adviser ran 2 scenarios. In the first, Marcus did nothing different and Jennifer received the death benefit as a lump sum. On the taxable component of approximately $940,000, Jennifer would pay 15% tax — $141,000. In the second scenario, Marcus maximised his non-concessional contributions for the next 4 years (using the bring-forward rule where available), shifting the tax-free proportion from 33% to approximately 52%. Jennifer's tax bill on the same total death benefit: approximately $91,000. The difference: $50,000 — achieved through structuring, not speculation.

$50,000 Tax Saving Through Component Planning

By systematically increasing the tax-free component from 33% to 52% over 4 years of non-concessional contributions, Marcus reduced the potential death benefit tax liability for his adult daughter by $50,000.

Downsizer Contributions: Unlocking Equity for Retirement

One of the more generous superannuation law is the downsizer contribution — a provision allowing Australians aged 55 or over to contribute up to $300,000 (or $600,000 for couples) from the proceeds of selling their principal residence into superannuation, outside the normal contribution caps.

The rules are specific. The property must have been owned for at least 10 years. You (or your spouse) must have lived in it. The contribution must be made within 90 days of settlement. And crucially — it counts against your Transfer Balance Cap when moved into pension phase, but it does not count against your non-concessional contribution cap. This means members with a balance above $2 million (who would normally be unable to make non-concessional contributions) can still make a downsizer contribution.

The Downsizer Contribution — Key Requirements

• Age 55+ at time of contribution • Property owned for at least 10 years • Property was or is your principal residence • Contribution within 90 days of settlement • Maximum $300,000 per eligible person ($600,000 per couple) • Does not count toward NCC cap but does count toward TBC on pension commencement • Can only be used once per person • Must notify the fund in writing using the approved ATO form

Peter and Carolyn: The $600,000 Downsizer Strategy

Peter and Carolyn were 68 and 65 respectively. They sold their family home of 32 years in Sydney's inner west for $2.85 million. Their SMSF had approximately $1.4 million. Neither had previously used the downsizer contribution.

On the advice of their planner, each made a $300,000 downsizer contribution into the SMSF within 90 days of settlement (a timeframe the ATO can extend in limited cases). The fund's total balance rose to around $2.0 million. They used $900,000 from the proceeds to purchase a smaller home, eliminating the mortgage worry that had nagged at Peter for years.

The $600,000 contributed attracted no contributions tax, and importantly downsizer contributions don't count towards concessional or non-concessional contribution caps. Each member then commenced an account-based pension with their portion. To the extent those amounts support retirement-phase pensions, the fund's earnings on that capital can be exempt from tax under the ECPI rules—which is why downsizer contributions can materially improve after-tax retirement outcomes compared with holding the same investments outside super.

> **$117,000 Estimated Tax Saving – Downsizer Strategy**
>
> By contributing $600,000 downsizer proceeds into their SMSF and commencing pensions, Peter and Carolyn estimated $117,000 in tax savings over a 15-year retirement at 6% returns.

Super Splitting: Equalising for the Transfer Balance Cap

Many couples have uneven superannuation balances — a common legacy of years when one partner worked full-time while the other worked part-time or took career breaks for caring responsibilities. This inequality can create a specific retirement problem: if one partner accumulates a much larger balance, they may approach or exhaust their transfer balance cap, while the other partner's cap remains underused.

Contribution splitting allows a member to request that their super fund transfer to their spouse up to 85% of their taxed splitable concessional contributions for a financial year (generally the lesser of 85% of concessional contributions and the concessional contributions cap). Non-concessional contributions cannot be split, and eligibility rules apply to the receiving spouse based on age and retirement status.

The strategy is most powerful when started early. Where one partner consistently receives higher employer contributions and/or salary sacrifice contributions, regular splitting over 15–20 years can materially equalise balances — increasing the couple's ability to move more of their combined super into retirement phase, where earnings may be exempt from tax (subject to each person's transfer balance cap).

Salary Sacrifice: The Tool That Rewards Precision

Salary sacrifice is the most commonly used mechanism for making concessional contributions above the employer Superannuation Guarantee. An employee agrees with their employer to forgo a portion of pre-tax salary, which the employer pays directly to the employee's superannuation fund as an additional employer contribution.

For SMSF members, the arrangement must be effective — meaning it must be agreed in writing before the salary is earned. It can't be backdated to amounts already earned or accrued.

Three common mistakes in salary sacrifice arrangements deserve specific mention. First: total concessional contributions (SG + salary sacrifice + any other concessional amounts) must be managed against the $30,000 concessional cap (2025–26), unless you're eligible to use unused cap amounts under the carry-forward rules. I have seen high-income earners set up salary sacrifice at $2,500 per month without realising their employer was already paying $24,000 in SG annually, leaving them a cap of only $6,000. Second: salary sacrifice does not always reduce income for government benefits. Many means tests use adjusted taxable income, which often adds back reportable employer super contributions (including salary sacrifice), so the expected benefit impact can be neutral or even adverse depending on the payment. Third: salary sacrifice agreements should be reviewed annually when the $30,000 cap or the employer SG rate changes.

The Catch-Up Contribution: 5 Years of Accumulation

Since July 1, 2018, members with a Total Superannuation Balance below $500,000 at June 30 of the prior year have been able to carry forward unused concessional contribution cap space from the previous 5 years. If you made only $15,000 in concessional contributions in a given year (against a cap of $27,500 at the time), the unused $12,500 can potentially be used in a future year.

This provision is particularly valuable for members who took career breaks, worked part-time, or experienced periods of lower income. It provides an opportunity to accelerate the accumulation of tax-advantaged retirement savings in higher-income years. Consult the ATO's online services or your adviser to confirm exactly how much unused cap is available in your specific case — the calculation is individual and time-sensitive.

Chapter Seven: The Essential Principles

Contributions and withdrawals are the metabolism of your SMSF — the ongoing flow of resources in and out that sustains the structure over decades. Getting these flows right requires understanding not just the rules that apply today, but which rules will apply at which ages, under which circumstances. The rules that govern a 45-year-old are not the rules that will govern you at67.

Principle	The Risk of Ignoring It
From age 67, document the work test if claiming a deduction for personal contributions	ATO may disallow contributions if hours worked cannot be demonstrated
Check TSB before large non-concessional contributions	Excess NCC tax at 47% if you inadvertently contribute above your available cap
Avoid in-specie transfers of residential property from members/related parties	Generally prohibited under SIS s 66 (exceptions are narrow)
Plan Transfer Balance Cap allocation carefully at pension commencement	Excess transfer balance tax and permanent loss of full ECPI benefit on the excess
Ensure minimum pension payments are made before June 30	Loss of ECPI exemption for entire year — potentially $50K–$200K+ in unexpected tax
Initiate contributions at least 5 business days before deadline	Settlement date risk; contribution may fall in wrong financial year
Review salary sacrifice arrangements annually	Risk of exceeding concessional cap; downstream effects on assessable income
Understand proportional rule for death benefits	Non-dependent beneficiaries taxed on taxable component — structuring can reduce this

Steven Li learned the 28 day allocation rule the hard way — through an audit and a $31,000 cost he could have avoided by initiating his June contribution 10 days earlier. Emily learned the deemed disposal rule through a $60,750 tax bill she had not budgeted for. Richard Hartley learned the Transfer Balance Cap through an excess contribution tax of $47,000 and a $143,000 forward cost he will never recover.

Their stories are not cautionary tales about inadequate intelligence or careless attitudes. They are stories about the very specific kind of expertise this area demands. The contribution and withdrawal rules are technical, interconnected, and age-dependent. No single conversation with an adviser — however competent — is sufficient to absorb all of them once and remember them forever.

What works is a system: an annual contribution review meeting with your adviser every May, in which you confirm your contribution year-to-date, your remaining cap space, your work test eligibility (if making deductible personal contributions at ages 67–74), and your planned contributions for the remaining weeks of the financial year. 45 minutes in April can prevent the loss of tens of thousands of dollars in the following year.

In the next chapter, we will address the most emotionally charged topic in all of superannuation law: what happens to your SMSF when you die.

The Superannuation Government Co-Contribution: A Forgotten Benefit for Lower-Income Years

In the focus on large concessional and non-concessional contribution strategies, a genuinely valuable government benefit is frequently overlooked: the superannuation government co-contribution. For eligible individuals, the government matches personal after-tax contributions to superannuation at a rate of fifty cents per dollar, up to a maximum co-contribution of $500 per year. It is, in the most literal sense, free money — and it is systematically underutilised by people who could benefit from it.

The co-contribution is income-tested. For the 2025-26 financial year, the full $500 co-contribution is available to individuals with income below $45,400. It phases out progressively, reaching0 at approximately $60,400. For members with significant superannuation balances who nonetheless have a low-income year — perhaps due to a period of reduced work, a career transition, or taking time as a primary carer — the co-contribution can represent a meaningful additional benefit at minimal cost.

The mechanics are straightforward: make an after-tax (non-concessional) personal contribution to your superannuation fund, lodge your tax return, and the ATO automatically calculates and pays the co-contribution directly to your fund if you are eligible. No application form. No complex calculations. Just a contribution and a tax return.

For SMSF members, the co-contribution is available on the same terms as for any other superannuation fund member. The contribution must be made from after-tax income (employment income, business income, or other assessable income). Investment income, rental income, and capital gains do not qualify for the purpose of calculating co-contribution eligibility.

The Low Income Superannuation Tax Offset (LISTO)

For individuals earning $37,000 or less per year, there is a further government superannuation benefit: the Low Income Superannuation Tax Offset (LISTO). Under this scheme, the ATO effectively refunds the 15% contributions tax on concessional contributions up to $500 per year. The intent is to ensure that low-income earners are not disadvantaged by the superannuation tax system — which would otherwise tax their employer contributions at 15% when their personal marginal tax rate is lower.

For a trustee or member with a low-income year, the combination of the LISTO and the co-contribution can add up to $1,000 in government support to superannuation in a single financial year, at0 additional cost. These are small amounts relative to the scale of SMSF management, but they represent the kind of systematic, low-effort optimisation that distinguishes engaged trustees from passive ones.

Spouse Contributions: The Often-Overlooked Rebalancing Tool

The spouse contribution allows a higher-income member to contribute to their lower-income spouse's superannuation and receive a personal tax offset. For the 2025-26 financial year, contributing up to $3,000 to a spouse's superannuation fund (when the spouse's income is below $37,000) attracts an 18% tax offset for the contributing spouse — a maximum tax reduction of $540.

The financial benefit of the offset is modest. The strategic benefit, however, can be substantial. Spouse contributions, particularly when combined with contribution splitting, allow couples to progressively equalise their superannuation balances over time. And as we discussed in the main chapter text, an equalised balance between 2 members produces a significantly better Transfer Balance Cap outcome at retirement than a lopsided distribution.

Consider a couple where one partner earns $200,000 and the other earns $35,000. The higher earner's superannuation balance grows rapidly from employer contributions and salary sacrifice. The lower earner's grows slowly. Without intervention, the couple may arrive at retirement with an eighty/ten split between the 2 members' balances — the higher earner's balance exceeding the Transfer Balance Cap, the lower earner's largely untapped. With consistent spouse contributions and contribution splitting over 15 years, the split can approach fifty/fifty — allowing both members to utilise their full Transfer Balance Cap and potentially sheltering an additional $2 million in tax-free pension phase.

The Concessional Contribution: Tax Agent or Trustee — Who Claims the Deduction?

For self-employed SMSF members and employees making personal after-tax contributions that they intend to treat as concessional (and claim as a tax deduction), there is a critical procedural requirement that is frequently overlooked: the notice of intent to claim a deduction.

Before lodging your tax return, you must serve a written notice on your SMSF trustee that you intend to claim a deduction for the personal contribution you have made. The trustee must acknowledge receipt. Only after this process is completed is the deduction valid. If you lodge your tax return claiming the deduction before serving the notice — or if you serve the notice after the deduction is already claimed — the deduction may be disallowed.

This sounds like a minor administrative step. For the self-employed SMSF member who is also their own trustee, it feels almost absurdly circular — you are notifying yourself. But the law requires the step, and it requires it to be done in the correct order. Many accounting software packages now automate the process, but it is worth confirming explicitly with your accountant each year that the notice has been served and acknowledged in the correct sequence.

> **Notice of Intent to Claim — The Sequence That Must Be Followed**
>
> 1. Make the personal contribution to your SMSF. 2. Before lodging your tax return, serve a valid written Notice of Intent

> to Claim a Deduction on the trustee. 3. Receive written acknowledgement from the trustee. 4. Lodge your tax return claiming the deduction. If the sequence is broken — if you lodge your tax return before serving the notice, or serve the notice after an amendment is not possible — the deduction is lost. On a $30,000 concessional contribution at a 47% marginal rate, the lost deduction costs $14,100.

Division 293 Tax: The High-Income Earner's Concessional Contribution Surcharge

For individuals with combined income and concessional contributions above $250,000 per year, an additional 15% tax applies to concessional contributions. This is called Division 293 tax, and it effectively eliminates the tax advantage of making concessional contributions for very high earners — raising their effective contribution tax rate from 15% to 30%, which is the corporate tax rate, making concessional contributions no more (or less) advantageous than income drawn as salary.

Division 293 is assessed to the individual (not the fund). The ATO issues the assessment, and the individual can pay it from personal funds or elect to release an amount from super under the ATO's release authority process

For SMSF members near the $250,000 threshold — particularly where income fluctuates or where salary sacrifice and carry-forward concessional caps are being considered — it is worth modelling Division 293 outcomes before finalising contributions. In some cases, shifting the mix between concessional and non-concessional contributions may be sensible, depending on the person's caps and goals.

Income Level	Concessional Contribution Tax Rate	Effective Tax Saving vs Top Marginal Rate (47%)

Under $250,000 combined	15%	32% saving per dollar contributed
Over $250,000 combined	30% (15% + Division 293)	17% saving per dollar contributed

The interaction between salary sacrifice, concessional contributions, and Division 293 is one of the most technically complex areas of superannuation planning for high-income earners. It requires annual modelling that accounts for the specific year's income, the current contribution cap, the member's total superannuation balance, and any unused carry-forward cap space. This is not an area for guesswork or 'approximately right' calculations. The difference between an optimised and a sub-optimal contribution strategy at this income level can easily exceed $10,000 in a single year.

Chapter 8
When the Trustee Dies

Death Benefits, Binding Nominations, and the Inheritance Questions You Haven't Asked

Nobody wants to spend an afternoon thinking about their own death. I understand this viscerally, having watched clients physically recoil from the topic in the same way they might recoil from an unpleasant medical diagnosis. The instinct is to change the subject, to address it 'later,' to trust that things will somehow sort themselves out.

What I have seen in 10 years of practice is that they rarely do — not without deliberate planning. The families I have watched navigate the death of a superannuation trustee fall, with depressing regularity, into 2 categories: those who had done the planning and experienced grief uncomplicated by financial catastrophe, and those who had not and experienced both.

Chapter Eight is about the planning that separates those 2 categories. It is about what happens to your SMSF when you die, who gets to decide where the money goes, how it is taxed, and how a single document — or the absence of one — can either protect your family's financial future or fracture it.

This chapter contains three stories. Arthur's is a story about trustee discretion — the most powerful and most misused feature of superannuation death benefits. Patrick's is a story about tax — specifically, the enormous and frequently overlooked tax exposure that affects non-dependent beneficiaries. And the story of Robert and his wife Carol is the template: the careful, deliberate planning that made a $3.8 million estate transfer clean, efficient, and exactly as Robert intended.

How Death Benefits Work in an SMSF: The Basic Framework

When a member of an SMSF dies, their superannuation benefit does not automatically form part of their estate and pass under their will. Superannuation sits outside the estate. It is governed by the superannuation legislation, the trust deed, and — critically — any binding death benefit nomination the deceased member made during their lifetime.

The death benefit must be paid to one or more 'eligible beneficiaries.' The legislation defines these as: the member's dependants (including their spouse, children under eighteen, financially dependent children, interdependency relationship partners, and any other financial dependants), or the member's legal personal representative (LPR), who will incorporate the benefit into the estate and distribute it under the will.

If there is no valid binding nomination — or if the nomination has lapsed — the surviving trustees have discretion to pay the benefit to any eligible beneficiary, in whatever proportions they choose. This discretion is not subject to the deceased's wishes as expressed in a will or in a letter of wishes. It belongs entirely to the remaining trustees.

> **The Three Paths for Death Benefits**
>
> 1. Binding Death Benefit Nomination (BDBN): Trustee must follow the deceased's instructions — no discretion permitted. 2. Non-Binding Nomination: Trustee takes member's preference into account but retains discretion. 3. No Nomination: Trustee has full discretion to pay any eligible beneficiary in any proportion.

Arthur's Story: Trustee Discretion and the Ex-Wife Who Wasn't Expecting It

Arthur was 67, had been divorced for 14 years, and had been in a new relationship with a woman named Denise for the past 9 years. They shared a home but had never married. Arthur had two adult children from his first marriage — a son, Thomas, aged 41, and a daughter, Rebecca, aged 38.

Arthur had $1.2 million in his SMSF. He had made a non-binding death benefit nomination in favour of his estate about 6 years earlier, with a note on the form that he wanted the benefit to go to Thomas and Rebecca equally. When he signed the form, he believed — not unreasonably, given the language — that this constituted a clear instruction. He did not revisit it.

In 2021, Arthur died unexpectedly from a cardiac event. Denise, who was also a member of the SMSF — both had joined the fund together several years before — became the sole remaining trustee. She was grief-stricken. She was also, as it transpired, the surviving trustee of a fund that held $1.2 million she now had discretion to distribute.

Denise had not been financially provided for under Arthur's will, which had been drafted before they met and which Arthur had repeatedly intended to update but never did. Faced with the prospect of losing the home they shared — Arthur's estate was not large enough to allow Denise to continue living there without liquidating the property — Denise exercised her trustee discretion and paid the entire $1.2 million to herself as Arthur's de facto partner.

She was legally entitled to do this. Denise met the definition of a dependant — a person in an interdependency relationship with Arthur. The payment was not unlawful. But it was not what Arthur had intended, not what his children had expected, and not what Arthur had understood his 'non-binding nomination' would produce. Thomas and Rebecca received nothing from the superannuation.

> **$1,200,000 Arthur's Children Received Nothing from the SMSF**
>
> A non-binding nomination, a surviving-trustee with legitimate discretion, and an outdated will combined to redirect $1.2 million away from the intended beneficiaries. Arthur's adult children received $0 from superannuation.

I have changed names throughout this story, but the essential facts are taken from a real case pattern I have encountered multiple times. The legal result is always the same. The human result varies — sometimes the family reaches an accommodation, sometimes the matter proceeds to court on the grounds of undue influence or breach of trustee duties, sometimes the children simply accept it. But the outcome that Arthur intended — an equal distribution to Thomas and Rebecca — was never achievable once the non-binding nomination was the governing document and Denise was the surviving trustee.

The Binding Death Benefit Nomination: What It Is and Why It Matters

A Binding Death Benefit Nomination (BDBN) is a formal instruction to the trustee that must be followed if it is validly made. A valid BDBN removes trustee discretion entirely. If Arthur had executed a valid BDBN nominating Thomas and Rebecca as beneficiaries in equal shares, Denise as the surviving trustee would have had no choice but to pay the benefit as instructed.

The operative word is 'validly.' A BDBN is only binding if it meets all the formal requirements of the trust deed and the legislation. Those requirements typically include: the nomination being in writing, signed by the member, witnessed by 2 adults who are not beneficiaries, and served on the trustee. Many trust deeds also require that the BDBN be renewed every 3 years, or it lapses and reverts to non-binding status.

Type of Nomination	Trustee Discretion	Lapse Risk	What Happens at Death
Binding Death Benefit Nomination (BDBN)	None — must follow	Yes — typically 3 years unless non-lapsing	Benefit paid exactly as nominated

Non-Lapsing BDBN	None — must follow	No — valid until changed or cancelled	Benefit paid exactly as nominated, indefinitely
Non-Binding Nomination	Full discretion	No formal lapse	Nomination considered but not binding; trustee decides
No Nomination	Full discretion	N/A	Trustee pays any eligible beneficiary in any proportion
Reversionary Pension	Automatically reverting	N/A — not a nomination	Pension reverts to nominated reversionary beneficiary automatically

The three-year renewal requirement is, in my practice, the single most commonly overlooked element of death benefit planning. I have reviewed SMSF files where a BDBN was meticulously drafted, properly executed, witnessed correctly — and then left untouched for 5 or 7 years. By the time of the member's death, it had long since lapsed. The surviving trustee now had full discretion. The careful planning of a decade prior was void.

My standard recommendation is to calendar BDBN renewals 2 months before the three-year anniversary — not on the anniversary, but before it, to allow time for any required consultation, drafting, or execution. And where the trust deed permits non-lapsing BDBNs, I strongly recommend considering this option for members with clear, stable estate planning intentions.

Who Can Be a Beneficiary Under a BDBN?

A BDBN can only direct benefits to eligible beneficiaries — specifically, a dependant or the legal personal representative (LPR), a dependant includes a spouse, children of any age (including adult children), a person in an interdependency relationship, or a person who was financially dependent on the member. You cannot nominate a friend, sibling (unless financially dependent), or a charity directly under a BDBN.

To benefit a non-dependant individual or entity, you must nominate your LPR, and the superannuation benefit will then be distributed via your estate in accordance with your will.

This creates an important interplay between your BDBN and your will. If you want your superannuation death benefit to flow to your estate for distribution under your will, you must nominate the LPR. But this also exposes the benefit to potential estate challenges — contested wills, family provision claims — that a direct BDBN to a dependant would avoid.

If you want certainty that the benefit reaches a specific dependant without the risk of an estate challenge, you nominate that dependant directly in the BDBN. If you want flexibility — particularly if your family structure involves dependants and non-dependants and the distribution is complex — you nominate the LPR and ensure your will is current and carefully drafted.

Patrick's Story: The Tax Trap That Cost His Son $135,000

Patrick was 69, widowed, with a son named James aged 42. James had a family, a mortgage, and a successful career as a civil engineer. Patrick had always intended to leave everything he had to James. His SMSF had $900,000 when Patrick died — entirely in accumulation phase, as Patrick had not yet commenced a pension.

Patrick's estate — his house, his bank accounts, his share portfolio outside superannuation — passed to James through the will, free of inheritance tax (Australia has no inheritance tax on estate assets). Patrick had assumed, reasonably but incorrectly, that his superannuation death benefit would be treated the same way.

It was not.

The Superannuation Death Benefit Tax: A Hidden Inheritance Tax

Australia may not have a formal inheritance tax, but it has something that functions very similarly for non-dependent adult beneficiaries receiving superannuation death benefits. When a superannuation death benefit is paid to a non-dependant — and adult children over 18 are not dependants for superannuation tax purposes unless they are financially dependent on the deceased — the taxable component of the benefit is taxed at 15% (plus the Medicare levy of 2%), giving an effective rate of 17%.

Patrick's $900,000 was approximately 40% tax-free component ($360,000) and 60% taxable component ($540,000). James, as a non-dependent adult child, paid 17% tax on the $540,000 taxable component — a tax bill of $91,800.

Had Patrick commenced an account-based pension before he died and nominated James as beneficiary under a BDBN to the LPR — allowing the benefit to flow through the estate — the tax treatment would have been identical. The tax on the taxable component is assessed regardless of how the benefit is received, whether as a lump sum directly or through the estate.

> **$91,800 Patrick's Son Paid 17% Tax on $540,000 Taxable Component**
>
> Australia's de facto inheritance tax on superannuation: non-dependent beneficiaries (including adult children) pay 17% (15% + Medicare levy) on the taxable component. On a $540,000 taxable component, that was $91,800.

Could this have been reduced? Yes — and this is perhaps the most important planning point in this chapter. The proportion of tax-free versus taxable component in superannuation is not fixed. It is the cumulative result of contributions made during the member's lifetime. Non-concessional contributions (after-tax contributions) create tax-free component. Concessional contributions and investment earnings create taxable component. If Patrick had made non-concessional contributions throughout his accumulation phase — steadily building the tax-free proportion — the tax burden on James at death would have been lower.

Strategies to Reduce Death Benefit Tax for Non-Dependants

The most effective strategies for reducing death benefit tax on non-dependant beneficiaries are those that increase the tax-free proportion of the superannuation balance over time. Given the proportional rule, every dollar contributed as a non-concessional contribution increases the tax-free component on a dollar-for-dollar basis. The following table illustrates the difference that a higher tax-free proportion makes on a $900,000 death benefit.

Tax-Free Proportion	Tax-Free Component	Taxable Component	Tax on Death Benefit (17%)
20%	$180,000	$720,000	$122,400
40%	$360,000	$540,000	$91,800
60%	$540,000	$360,000	$61,200
80%	$720,000	$180,000	$30,600
100%	$900,000	$0	$0

Achieving a 100% tax-free position requires that all accumulation have come from non-concessional contributions — an unusual and typically impractical position. But moving from 40% tax-free to 70% or 80% tax-free, through years of deliberate non-concessional contribution strategy, can meaningfully reduce the eventual tax exposure for beneficiaries who are not dependants.

A second strategy — available only to members in retirement phase — is the pension recontribution strategy. A member who has commenced a pension can withdraw a lump sum completely tax-free, and recontribute the full proceeds as a non-concessional contribution. Each dollar recontributed is, by definition, tax-free component. For members with capacity for non-concessional contributions, this strategy carries no immediate tax cost and can significantly alter the death benefit tax profile at no expense to the member.

Reversionary Pensions: The Automatic Survivor Option

For married or partnered trustees, a reversionary pension is often the most elegant death benefit mechanism. When a member nominates a reversionary beneficiary for their account-based pension, the pension does not cease at the member's death — it automatically 'reverts' to the nominated beneficiary, who continues receiving the pension payments without any need for trustee decision-making.

The reversionary beneficiary must be a dependant — typically a spouse. They inherit the pension, including its associated transfer balance cap implications. There is a twelve-month grace period during which the reversionary pension does not count against the surviving spouse's Transfer Balance Cap — giving time to plan any required commutation.

The tax treatment for a reversionary pension paid to a spouse is entirely tax-free if both the member and beneficiary are over 60. For those under 60, the relevant pension tax rules apply.

Robert's Story: The Architecture of a Perfect Plan

Robert Ashworth was 64 when I first met him. His SMSF held $3.8 million — a diversified portfolio built over 22 years of careful accumulation and investment. His wife, Carol, was 61 and also a member of the fund. They had two adult children: Natalie, 37, and Michael, 34. Both children were self-supporting professionals and were not financially dependent on Robert or Carol.

Robert's goal was simple in its expression, complex in its execution: he wanted to ensure that every dollar he had worked to accumulate ended up where he intended, with as little tax as possible, and with zero possibility of dispute or ambiguity. He had watched a business colleague's estate dissolve in litigation after a poorly structured superannuation plan and had resolved that this would not happen to his family.

Layer One: The Reversionary Pension for Carol

Robert had a pension balance of $2 million — his full Transfer Balance Cap. Carol had a pension balance of $900,000, having taken a seven-year career break when the children were young. Robert nominated Carol as the reversionary beneficiary of his pension. If Robert were to die first, Carol would automatically receive the $2 million pension — continuing the same pension he had been drawing, without any trustee decision required.

Carol's Transfer Balance Cap at that point had $1.1 million of unused space ($2M cap minus her existing $900,000 pension). The $2 million reversionary pension would exceed her cap by $900,000. Under the rules, Carol had 12 months from Robert's death to commute the excess back into accumulation phase. The accumulation balance would pay 15% tax on earnings — not zero — but this was far better than having no plan at all.

We modelled both the commutation scenario and an alternative where Robert reduced his pension balance (through lump sum withdrawals) in advance of death to bring the reversionary pension amount within Carol's remaining TBC space. Robert elected the lump sum withdrawal strategy — drawing down approximately $1.1 million over 3 years and distributing it to an investment account in Carol's name. This reduced the reversionary pension to approximately $900,000, well within Carol's available TBC space.

> **$900,000 Robert's Restructured Reversionary Pension**
>
> By drawing down his pension by $1.1M over 3 years before death, Robert's reversionary pension of $900,000 fit comfortably within Carol's remaining $1.1M Transfer Balance Cap space — eliminating the excess TBC problem entirely.

Layer Two: The Binding Nomination for Natalie and Michael

Carol's superannuation balance — $900,000 in pension — also required careful planning. If Carol outlived Robert, what would happen at Carol's death? The potential beneficiaries were Natalie and Michael, neither of whom was a dependant. Without a BDBN, Carol's surviving trustee (at that point, whoever was co-trustee with Carol after Robert's death — they used a corporate trustee structure) would have discretion.

Carol executed a non-lapsing BDBN nominating her legal personal representative. Her will was drafted to leave the estate — including the superannuation death benefit flowing through the LPR — equally to Natalie and Michael. The will included a specific testamentary trust for each child, providing significant tax-efficiency benefits for the grandchildren's education expenses and offering protection from any future relationship property claims against Natalie or Michael.

The tax on the taxable component of Carol's balance, paid by Natalie and Michael as non-dependants, would be unavoidable. But the proportion of tax-free component in Carol's fund had been substantially increased through the non-concessional contributions she had made during the recontribution strategy years. The estimated tax on death benefit: approximately $47,000 — substantially less than the $120,000+ that a lower tax-free proportion would have generated.

Layer Three: The Corporate Trustee Structure

Perhaps the most critical structural element of Robert and Carol's plan was their use of a corporate trustee. When Robert died, the corporate trustee company continued to hold the SMSF assets without any interruption. There was no scramble to appoint a new individual trustee, no temporary loss of legal capacity over the fund, no freeze on asset transactions during the estate administration period. The corporate trustee, with Carol as the sole director, continued managing the fund seamlessly.

Under an individual trustee structure, Robert's death would have triggered a requirement to appoint a new trustee within a specified period or wind up the fund. During that period, the fund's ability to transact could be constrained. Assets might need to be sold in unfavourable market conditions. The administrative burden on Carol — already grieving — would have been substantial.

Corporate trustees cost more to establish and maintain. But for couples building significant SMSF wealth together, the continuity advantage at the death of one trustee is, in my view, worth every dollar of the additional cost.

Structure	On Death of 1 Trustee	Continuity	Cost
Individual trustees (members as trustees)	Must appoint replacement or wind up within specified period; potential asset freeze	Poor	Low setup
Corporate trustee (company)	Director change only; fund continues uninterrupted	Excellent	Higher setup ($1,000–$2,500 annually)

The Legal Personal Representative: Superannuation's Bridge to the Estate

The Legal Personal Representative — the executor of the estate or the administrator if there is no will — occupies a unique and sometimes confusing position in superannuation death benefit planning. When a member nominates the LPR as the beneficiary of a BDBN, they are not nominating a person. They are nominating an office — whoever holds the role of LPR at the time of death.

This distinction matters for 2 reasons. First, if the executor you intend to nominate predeceases you or is unable to act, a substitute executor (or court-appointed administrator) will take on the LPR role. The benefit still flows to the LPR — whoever that ultimately is. Second, the LPR has a dual identity in superannuation: they act both as a beneficiary (in that they receive the benefit) and as a representative of the estate (in that they hold the benefit on behalf of the estate's ultimate beneficiaries). The tax treatment depends on who the estate's ultimate beneficiaries are — dependants or non-dependants.

> **The LPR Dual Role — Why It Matters for Tax**
>
> When superannuation flows to the LPR, the tax treatment is assessed not on the LPR personally but on who the estate's beneficiaries are. If the estate's beneficiaries are all dependants (e.g., a spouse), the death benefit component that flows to them is treated as tax-free. If some beneficiaries are non-dependants (adult children), the taxable component flowing to them attracts the 17% tax. Ensure your will and superannuation nominations are aligned.

Testamentary Trusts: The Smart Container for Inherited Superannuation

Where superannuation death benefits are directed to the estate and then to adult beneficiaries, testamentary trusts offer a sophisticated tax-planning vehicle. A testamentary trust is a trust created by a will that comes into existence only at the testator's death. Assets flowing into the testamentary trust — including superannuation death benefits that have passed through the estate — can be distributed to trust beneficiaries (including minor children) at their individual tax rates.

The particular advantage: minor beneficiaries of testamentary trusts are taxed on trust income at adult tax rates rather than the 'children's tax' rate that normally applies to minors receiving investment income. This can substantially reduce the annual tax burden where superannuation death benefits are invested for grandchildren's benefit.

The testamentary trust must be established in the will before death. It cannot be created retrospectively. And the superannuation death benefit must be directed to the LPR — not directly to a beneficiary — for it to flow into the testamentary trust. Direct BDBN nominations to named individuals bypass the estate entirely and cannot be re-routed into a testamentary trust.

Challenging a BDBN: Is It Possible?

A validly executed BDBN is very difficult to challenge. It can be invalidated if it does not meet the formal requirements of the trust deed (improper witnessing, expired lapse period, directed to an ineligible beneficiary), if it can be shown that the member lacked capacity at the time of execution, or if it was obtained by undue influence.

Court challenges to BDBNs are typically expensive, uncertain, and time-consuming. They are not a reliable safety net for family members who feel they were treated unfairly. The cost of challenging a superannuation death benefit distribution can easily equal or exceed the amount being disputed, particularly for mid-sized funds.

This is another argument for getting the planning right in advance. A properly constructed BDBN, regularly reviewed and renewed, is far more durable than any number of handwritten letters of wishes, informal promises, or 'understandings' among family members.

The SMSF Trustee's Death Benefit Checklist

In closing, I offer the practical checklist I walk every client through when reviewing their death benefit planning. Not every item will be relevant to every reader. But working through this list — honestly and with professional support — is the single most important thing you can do to protect your family from the consequences of inadequate planning.

Action Item	Status to Confirm
BDBN in place and within 3-year validity period	Confirm date of last execution; calendar renewal reminder
BDBN directed to eligible beneficiaries only (dependants or LPR)	Verify each named beneficiary qualifies under current definitions
Trust deed permits non-lapsing BDBN (if desired)	Check deed; amend if needed before BDBN is executed
Reversionary pension nominated for spouse/partner (where applicable)	Pension commencement documents confirm reversionary nominee
Reversionary pension within surviving spouse's TBC space	Model TBC usage before and after death; commute excess in advance if needed
Will current and consistent with superannuation nominations	Confirm will reflects same intent as BDBN/reversionary nomination
Corporate trustee in place (for couples especially)	Corporate trustee registered and operative
Tax-free vs taxable component proportion reviewed	NCC strategy in place to improve ratio for non-dependent beneficiaries

Testamentary trusts in will (if adult non-dependent children are beneficiaries)	Will drafter has included testamentary trust provisions
All trustees know where BDBN and trust deed documents are held	Documents in secure, accessible location known to all trustees and executor

Arthur did not have a binding nomination. His children received nothing. Patrick did not understand how the taxable component would affect his son. James paid $91,800 he did not need to pay. Robert did every item on this list. His estate transferred cleanly, at minimum tax cost, exactly as he intended.

The difference between these outcomes was not luck. It was planning — specific, documented, reviewed, renewed, and coordinated across the superannuation structure, the will, and the family's broader financial picture.

In the final chapter of the case study section, we turn to the last major decision any SMSF trustee will make: winding the fund up.

The Interdependency Relationship: Expanding the Dependant Definition

The category of 'dependant' for superannuation death benefit purposes is broader than many trustees realise. Beyond the obvious categories of spouse (including de facto partner) and financially dependent children, the legislation includes 'interdependency relationship' — a relationship of mutual emotional support, domestic connection, and financial interdependence that does not necessarily fit the traditional family structure.

Two people are in an interdependency relationship if: they have a close personal relationship; they live together; one or each of them provides the other with financial support; and one or each of them provides the other with domestic support and personal care. The relationship does not need to be sexual or romantic. Two adult siblings who have lived together for 10 years, one caring for the other through a chronic illness, may qualify. An adult child who has moved back home to care for an ageing parent may qualify. A long-term companion who shares a home and supports a member financially may qualify.

The practical significance: if you have a person in your life who is not a spouse or financial dependant in the traditional sense but with whom you have a relationship that meets the interdependency definition, that person may be eligible to receive a tax-free superannuation death benefit as a dependant. This has implications for both benefit planning and for the execution of your BDBN — specifically, whether to nominate that person directly or to direct the benefit through your estate.

> **Documenting an Interdependency Relationship**
>
> If you intend to nominate a person as your death benefit beneficiary on the basis of an interdependency relationship, document the relationship thoroughly during your lifetime: • Shared address records (lease agreements, rates notices, correspondence) • Evidence of mutual financial support (joint accounts, shared expenses) • Evidence of personal care arrangements • Statutory declaration by both parties describing the relationship At the time of death, the trustee must be satisfied that the relationship exists. Documentation provided in advance eliminates uncertainty and potential disputes.

Practical Timeline: Reviewing Your Death Benefit Plan

I close this expansion chapter with a practical recommendation on review frequency. Death benefit planning is not a one-time exercise. It is an ongoing discipline that requires periodic review as circumstances change. The following events should trigger an immediate review of your death benefit plan.

Triggering Event	Action Required
Marriage, de facto relationship commencement, or separation/divorce	Update BDBN; review reversionary pension nomination; review will
Birth of a child or grandchild	Assess whether child is a dependant; consider impact on estate distribution plan
Death of a nominated beneficiary	Update BDBN immediately; do not leave a nomination naming a deceased person
BDBN three-year anniversary approaching	Renew BDBN at least 60 days before expiry; check witnessing requirements
Significant increase in superannuation balance	Review whether tax-free component proportion is appropriate for non-dependent beneficiaries
Member approaching Transfer Balance Cap	Model reversionary pension impact; consider commutation in advance if needed
Acquisition of a corporate trustee	Confirm BDBN still valid under new trustee structure; review deed
Significant change to will	Ensure BDBN and will are consistent; review LPR nomination if applicable
Diagnosis of serious illness	Accelerate all review actions above; confirm all documents are accessible to nominees

None of these reviews is expensive or time-consuming. A single meeting with your SMSF adviser and estate planning solicitor, prompted by any of these triggers, is typically sufficient to update the relevant documents and ensure the plan remains current. The cost of not reviewing — the risk of an expired nomination, a lapsed BDBN, or a will that is no longer aligned with superannuation intentions — far exceeds the cost of the review.

Do the review. Put the reminder in your calendar now. Your family will be grateful, long after you are gone, that you thought of them clearly enough to act.

Chapter 9
The Art of the Exit

How to Wind Up Your SMSF Without Leaving Money on the Table — or Trouble in the Filing Cabinet

Every SMSF, without exception, will eventually come to an end. Some will wind up when the members retire and decide the administrative overhead is no longer justified. Some will wind up because a member's circumstances change — illness, overseas relocation, cognitive decline, the departure of a co-trustee whose presence was essential to the fund's operation. Some will wind up because the members simply decide, after careful consideration, that a retail or industry fund now serves their needs better than a self-managed structure.

None of these reasons is a failure. The purpose of an SMSF was never to exist in perpetuity — it was to serve its members optimally during the specific life stages when the self-managed structure added value. When that value proposition changes, winding up is not surrender. It is sound judgment.

What is a failure — and a surprisingly common one — is winding up badly. I have reviewed the files of dozens of SMSFs that closed, and the pattern of avoidable costs is remarkably consistent. CGT traps that could have been managed with 6 months' planning. Lost franking credits from poorly timed dividends. ECPI calculations that missed the fund's final year. Transfer timing errors that created unnecessary tax events. And, perhaps most painfully, emotional decisions made in haste during a difficult life transition — a divorce, an overseas move, a death — that cost tens of thousands of dollars because the trustee was managing grief or stress while simultaneously managing compliance.

Chapter Nine is about doing the exit well. We follow two stories — William and Patricia — whose wind-up experiences capture the most common and most costly mistakes. Then we walk through the 10-step wind-up process in the detail that the task demands.

Why SMSF Members Wind Up: The Common Triggers

Before the mechanics, it helps to understand the landscape. The reasons trustees choose to wind up their SMSFs cluster around a handful of recurring themes.

Reason for Wind-Up	Key Planning Consideration
Overseas relocation (member becomes non-resident)	SMSF may lose complying status if sole member non-resident; timing critical
Balance has fallen below cost-effective threshold	Compare annual SMSF costs vs retail/industry fee drag on current balance
Administrative complexity becomes unsustainable	Often triggered by health issues, cognitive decline, or loss of co-trustee
Death of a member (especially sole/primary member)	Wind-up may be required if surviving member cannot act as trustee
Relationship breakdown (co-trustee divorce)	Co-trustees may be unable to cooperate; winding up may be only solution
Investment strategy change (e.g., want diversified index funds only)	Industry fund may offer equivalent exposure at lower administrative cost
Loss of professional licence (some professions prohibit SMSF)	Must address promptly; regulatory breaches compound
Aged care transition	Complexity of managing SMSF during cognitive decline or full-time care

William's Story: The Overseas Move That Almost Cost Him $180,000

William Chang was 58 when he accepted a three-year secondment to Singapore with the multinational engineering firm he had worked for since graduating. He had spent 10 years building his SMSF — now worth $1.85 million — and he was enormously proud of it. His portfolio was a thoughtful mix of direct Australian shares, two commercial properties via LRBA, a global ETF through a managed account, and a modest cash allocation.

William's initial plan was straightforward: he would maintain the SMSF during his time in Singapore and continue managing it remotely. His wife, Christine, would remain in Australia. She was a co-trustee. William would continue in his advisory capacity from overseas. The investments were largely passive. What could go wrong?

The Residency Problem: When Your SMSF Becomes Non-Compliant

The ATO requires that an SMSF satisfy the 'residency conditions' to maintain its complying status — and therefore its concessional tax treatment. There are two main requirements relevant to William's situation. First: the fund must be 'established in Australia or holds assets in Australia.' This was satisfied. Second: the 'central management and control' of the fund must be ordinarily in Australia. The ATO defines 'central management and control' as the making of high-level decisions about the strategic direction of the fund — investment strategy, benefit policy, and so on.

If a trustee exercises central management and control from overseas, and if that trustee is out of Australia for more than 2 years, the ATO may determine that the fund's central management and control is outside Australia. The two-year period is a safe harbour — not an absolute rule. During that two-year period, the ATO generally accepts that central management and control can be temporarily exercised from overseas without compromising the fund's complying status. But William's secondment was for 3 years.

There was a further complication. For the 'active member' test, a fund with at least one active member is generally compliant. But the active member test has nuances that interact with non-resident status in ways that are not intuitively obvious. William's adviser initially assessed the situation as 'probably fine' because Christine was in Australia and could exercise central management and control. But the ATO's interpretation requires the active members to be Australian residents if the central management and control test is to be met by co-trustees. William, an active member, was not an Australian resident.

> **The SMSF Residency Test — Critical Conditions**
>
> An SMSF must meet 4 conditions to be a complying fund: 1. The fund was established in Australia, or assets held in Australia 2. Central management and control ordinarily in Australia (2-year overseas safe harbour) 3. If any assets are held — active members must be Australian residents 4. The ATO can still challenge if the arrangement appears designed to circumvent rules A non-complying SMSF is taxed at 45% on ALL income and assets. The cost is catastrophic.

When William's accountant finally ran the analysis 6 months into the secondment — William had delayed the review because of the chaos of relocating — the conclusion was unambiguous. Unless the situation was resolved, William's SMSF risked losing its complying status by the end of year two of his absence. A non-complying SMSF is assessed on its taxable income and net assets at 45%. On a fund worth $1.85 million, the potential tax exposure was terrifying.

> **Up to $832,500** **The Non-Compliance Tax Exposure William Faced**
>
> A non-complying SMSF is taxed at 45% on its entire taxable income and on the difference between the fund's assets and

> cost bases. On a $1.85M fund, worst-case tax exposure could approach $832,500.

The Solution: A Structured Wind-Up Before the Deadline

William and Christine decided to wind up the SMSF within the two-year safe harbour period — specifically, by the end of William's first year overseas. This gave them approximately 14 months to execute an orderly wind-up and transfer William's benefits to an industry fund that had no residency requirements. Christine would roll her benefits to the same industry fund initially, with a view to re-establishing an SMSF on their return to Australia.

The 14 months was, in retrospect, barely enough. The two commercial properties — held via LRBAs — required bank consent to sell or transfer, independent valuation for LRBA arm's length conditions, and substantial legal work. One property settled smoothly. The other had a sitting tenant with 8 months remaining on a fixed lease, which affected the sale price. The net sale proceeds were $140,000 less than the expected valuation, a shortfall partially attributable to the timing pressure they were under.

The direct shares were sold over 3 months. William's adviser carefully managed the realisation of gains against available capital losses, deferring where possible and timing disposals to minimise CGT. The global ETF was transferred in-specie to the industry fund — a permitted mechanism that avoided the CGT event of selling and rebuying.

Total costs of the wind-up: approximately $47,000 in legal fees, accounting fees, LRBA termination costs, and early sale discount. A significant number — but a fraction of what a non-compliant fund outcome would have cost. The lesson William drew from the experience: 'I should have started planning this on the day I accepted the job offer.'

$785,000 saved **Orderly Wind-Up vs Non-Compliance**

By winding up within the 2-year safe harbour rather than allowing the SMSF to become non-complying, William's family avoided up to $832,500 in potential tax, paying $47,000 in wind-up costs instead.

The Pre-Wind-Up Planning Window

William's case illustrates a principle I apply consistently: the planning for a wind-up should begin as soon as the trigger event is known, not when it has already occurred. The same is true for overseas relocations, imminent ill-health, divorce proceedings, or any other foreseeable event that will require a wind-up.

A minimum of 6 months is needed for a simple SMSF with liquid assets. 12 to 18 months is needed for a fund with property, LRBAs, or other illiquid or complex assets. 3 years is ideal for a fund that wants to wind up in an entirely tax-optimised fashion — selling assets gradually, managing CGT, harvesting losses, and timing final pension payments with precision.

The trustees who plan their wind-up 3 years before they want it to complete have the luxury of sequencing. They can sell assets in their most tax-efficient order. They can time CGT events across different financial years. They can maximise pension tax exemptions on gains made in the final years. The trustees who plan their wind-up in the month before they need it done have none of these options.

Patricia's Story: The CGT Trap Nobody Warned Her About

Patricia Nguyen was 67 and had been drawing a pension from her SMSF for 3 years. Her fund was straightforward: $980,000 in listed shares and ETFs, all in pension phase, all generating tax-exempt income under the ECPI rules. Patricia was a retired high school principal who had managed her SMSF diligently — until she decided, after considerable reflection, that the annual cost of $7,200 for accounting, audit, and ASIC fees was simply no longer justified now that her portfolio was entirely in index funds. She could achieve the same investment outcome through a low-cost industry fund for a fraction of the price.

Patricia engaged her accountant to manage the wind-up. The accountant, who was competent but not a superannuation specialist, advised her to sell the shares and ETFs over the course of the financial year and transfer the proceeds to the industry fund as a rollover. The proceeds from share sales would be tax-free under ECPI because the fund was in pension phase. The rollover would be tax-free as a superannuation transfer. A clean, simple exit.

What the accountant had not considered was the fund's choice of ECPI method.

The Segregated vs Unsegregated Trap at Wind-Up

Patricia's fund was entirely in pension phase — one hundred percent of the assets supported pension liabilities. Under the segregated ECPI method, all income and capital gains from those assets would be tax-exempt. Under the unsegregated method, an actuarial certificate would be required, and the exempt proportion would depend on the ratio of pension liabilities to total fund assets.

Patricia's fund had been using the segregated method since pension commencement. Under this method, capital gains realised when selling the shares were completely exempt — no tax applied. The accounts were clean.

The problem arose because Patricia had a balance in accumulation phase from a prior concessional contribution that her accountant had processed in July of the previous year — a delayed employer contribution that had been slow to come through. It was a small amount: $14,400. But it meant that for a portion of the financial year in which Patricia was winding up, her fund had both accumulation assets and pension assets. It was, technically, not fully in pension phase for the entire year.

The accountant, applying the strict interpretation of the segregated method rules, could not use the segregated method for that financial year — because the fund had accumulation assets during part of the year. The unsegregated method was required. The actuarial certificate produced an exempt percentage of 97.8% — because the accumulation assets were tiny relative to the total fund. But 2.2% of the capital gains realised on wind-up were taxable at 15%.

Patricia's capital gains during the wind-up year totalled approximately $412,000. 2.2% of $412,000 is $9,064. At 15% tax, the bill was $1,360. Small in absolute terms — but entirely avoidable, and a source of confusion and frustration that delayed the wind-up process by 4 months while the accounting firm sought clarity on the methodology.

The lesson here is not that the amount was catastrophic — it was not. The lesson is that even a 'simple' wind-up can produce unexpected tax consequences if the method choices and the fund's status for the entire financial year are not carefully audited before the wind-up process begins. For larger funds with more substantial gains, a similar methodological oversight could produce a six-figure tax bill.

> **$1,360 + 4-month delay** **Patricia's ECPI Method Oversight**
>
> A $14,400 accumulation contribution in the wind-up year required switching from segregated to unsegregated ECPI, creating an unexpected $1,360 tax bill and 4-month administrative delay on a $980K wind-up.

The 10-step Wind-Up Process

What follows is the structured process I recommend for every SMSF wind-up. The steps are sequential in some cases and parallel in others. The most important thing is not that you follow this list mechanically — it is that you begin early, engage specialists, and treat the wind-up with the same strategic seriousness you gave to the fund's establishment and ongoing management.

Step 1: Confirm the Wind-Up Decision and Review the Trust Deed

Before any action is taken, confirm that all trustees (and members) agree to wind up the fund. The trust deed specifies the process for making this decision — typically a resolution of trustees. Review the deed to ensure you follow the required process precisely. Some deeds require written resolutions; some require member consent in addition to trustee resolution. Failing to follow the deed's process can technically create an invalid wind-up, with consequent legal and tax complications.

Step 2: Notify the ATO

Once the decision to wind up is made, you are required to notify the ATO. This is done through the SMSF's registered tax agent or through the ATO's online services. The notification triggers the fund's final compliance obligations. It also means that from this point forward, the fund can no longer accept new contributions.

Step 3: Commission a Final Investment Strategy Review

Before beginning to sell assets, review the investment strategy with the specific objective of the wind-up in mind. The strategy should now prioritise liquidity, tax efficiency, and alignment with the target completion date. If you are selling direct property, this is the point at which to engage your real estate agent for an independent opinion on market timing and likely sale timeline.

Step 4: Address Binding Nominations and Pensions

If any member has an active account-based pension, this must be formally commuted before the fund can be wound up. The commutation converts the pension balance back to an accumulation (lump sum) benefit, which can then be rolled over or paid as a lump sum. Commutation triggers a reversal of the pension's transfer balance cap debit — an important technical detail that your adviser needs to account for in the TBC planning.

Update or cancel any binding death benefit nominations in writing. In a wind-up, these nominations become moot — but formal cancellation is cleaner than leaving them on the record.

Step 5: Sell or Transfer Assets

This is the operationally complex heart of the wind-up. Assets must be realised or transferred. The sequencing should be driven by tax efficiency.

For assets with capital gains: consider whether the gain can be realised in a financial year where other losses are available to offset, or whether timing the sale to straddle financial years is advantageous. Consider whether the fund's ECPI position allows the gain to be fully or partially exempt — and confirm this with an actuarial certificate if needed.

For direct property: ensure independent valuations are current. If an LRBA is in place, obtain bank consent well in advance of the target sale date — banks do not always move quickly.

For assets that can be transferred in-specie to the receiving fund: confirm whether the receiving fund accepts in-specie transfers (some do, some do not) and whether the transfer is tax-efficient. An in-specie transfer of listed shares may avoid a CGT event if the transferring fund is fully in pension phase.

Step 6: Complete the Final Annual Return

The SMSF must lodge a final SMSF annual return for the year in which the fund is wound up. This return should reflect all transactions, including the realisation of assets, final pension payments, and the rollover of member benefits. The return must be correct before the fund can be formally deregistered.

Step 7: Pay All Expenses and Liabilities

Before distributing any remaining assets, ensure that all outstanding expenses are paid — audit fees, accounting fees, LRBA termination costs, legal fees, any unpaid tax. The fund must have a zero or positive cash balance after paying expenses. Any remaining cash belongs to the members and is rolled over or paid out as their final benefit.

Step 8: Obtain the Final Audit

A final audit of the SMSF is required for the wind-up year. The auditor will review all transactions including the asset realisations, final benefit payments, and tax calculations. Engage your auditor early and provide complete records — the wind-up audit is often more complex than a standard annual audit.

Step 9: Roll Over or Pay Benefits

Once all liabilities are cleared and the final figures are confirmed, the member benefits are either rolled over to another superannuation fund or paid as lump sums (subject to the applicable conditions of release). Rollovers are made using ATO-approved rollover forms and must reference the receiving fund's details precisely. Benefits paid as lump sums generate PAYG withholding obligations that must be correctly calculated and reported.

Step 10: Cancel the Fund's ABN and Close the Bank Accounts

After the final return is lodged, benefits distributed, and the ATO has processed the wind-up notification, the fund's ABN is cancelled. Bank accounts associated with the SMSF should be closed. Any corporate trustee company should be deregistered with ASIC (if it will not continue to be used) or maintained as a dormant company if the members plan to re-establish an SMSF in the future.

Step	Action	Timing	Specialist Needed
1	Trustee resolution to wind up; review trust deed	Immediately	Solicitor (for deed review)
2	Notify ATO of wind-up decision	Within 28 days of resolution	Tax agent
3	Commission final investment strategy review	Concurrent with Step 2	Financial adviser
4	Commute pensions; update/cancel BDBNs	Before assets sold	Financial adviser, solicitor
5	Sell or transfer assets (tax-optimised sequencing)	3-18 months depending on assets	Financial adviser, real estate agent
6	Complete final annual return	By due date for wind-up year	Tax agent
7	Pay all expenses and liabilities	Before benefit distribution	Accountant
8	Obtain final audit	After financial year close	Approved SMSF auditor
9	Roll over or pay member benefits	After audit clearance	Tax agent, financial adviser
10	Cancel ABN; close bank accounts; deregister	After benefits distributed	ATO, ASIC, bank

	corporate trustee if applicable		

The Cost of a Wind-Up: What to Budget

Wind-up costs vary considerably depending on the complexity of the fund's assets. For a simple fund with only cash and listed securities, the process is relatively straightforward and costs are modest. For a fund with direct property, LRBAs, or other complex assets, the costs can be substantial.

Cost Component	Simple Fund (cash/ETFs only)	Complex Fund (property/LRBA)
Final accounting and tax agent fee	\$2,000 – \$4,000	\$4,000 – \$8,000
Final audit fee	\$1,000 – \$2,000	\$2,000 – \$4,000
Legal fees (trust deed, resolution documentation)	\$500 – \$1,500	\$2,000 – \$10,000+
LRBA termination costs (bank fees, discharge)	N/A	\$1,500 – \$5,000
Real estate agent commission (if direct property sold)	N/A	2%–3% of sale price
Corporate trustee deregistration (ASIC)	\$250	\$250
Rollover processing and receiving fund fees	Minimal	Minimal

Estimated total range	$4,000 – $8,000	$12,000 – $35,000+

Re-Establishing an SMSF After Wind-Up

Some members wind up their SMSF temporarily — due to overseas relocation, a period of simplified investing needs, or a major life transition — with the intention of re-establishing a fund at a later date. This is permissible. A new SMSF can be established at any time by eligible members. The previous fund's history is irrelevant; the new fund starts fresh.

However, there are costs to the stop-start approach. Each establishment involves legal fees, trust deed preparation, bank account opening, and ATO registration. Each wind-up involves the same. If the fund is likely to resume within 3 to 5 years, the cumulative cost of stopping and restarting may exceed the annual carrying cost of maintaining the fund in a dormant-but-compliant state — though this depends heavily on the fund's asset complexity.

When an SMSF Wind-Up Is Forced: Regulatory Non-Compliance

Most wind-ups are voluntary. But some are forced — triggered by a regulator determination that the fund is non-compliant and must be restructured or wound up. The ATO has the power to make a fund non-complying, which effectively imposes a punitive tax rate on all assets and income. It can also accept an enforceable undertaking from trustees (a formal commitment to remediate breaches) or, in extreme cases, pursue disqualification and criminal prosecution.

A forced wind-up is invariably more expensive, more stressful, and more damaging than a planned one. The assets may need to be sold at short notice. The tax consequences may be severe. The legal costs of responding to regulatory action can be substantial. And the reputational consequences — for members who are professionals or who hold fiduciary roles elsewhere — can be career-defining.

If you are a trustee who suspects your fund has compliance issues — unreported breaches, contributions errors, related party transactions that may not have been properly documented, or insurance that has lapsed — the right response is always to engage proactively with your adviser and, if needed, with the ATO's voluntary disclosure process. Voluntary disclosure, while not without cost, consistently produces better outcomes than being found in breach by an ATO audit.

Patricia and William: The Lessons in Summary

William's story demonstrates that timing is everything in a wind-up. The trigger event — in his case, an overseas secondment — created a hard deadline. Against that deadline, the planning had to be both technically rigorous (navigating residency rules, LRBA conditions, CGT management) and practically executable (engaging agents, banks, lawyers, and accountants across multiple time zones). Beginning 18 months before the deadline rather than 6 months would have eliminated the forced discount on the second property sale and reduced the legal bill significantly.

Patricia's story demonstrates that even small administrative imperfections can create complications. A $14,400 accumulation contribution in the wind-up year was invisible to anyone not specifically looking for it — and when found, it changed the fund's ECPI method, creating unexpected tax and a four-month delay. A thorough pre-wind-up audit — a comprehensive review of the fund's status, method choices, and outstanding issues — before the wind-up process begins is the insurance against these surprises.

Both stories affirm a principle that runs throughout this book: the complexity of an SMSF does not diminish when you decide to stop managing it. It concentrates. Every unresolved issue, every deferred decision, every assumption that was probably fine — all of it arrives at the wind-up in a compressed form that requires attention, expertise, and time. The trustees who give themselves that time leave well. The ones who don't, leave expensively.

> **The Wind-Up Principle**
>
> Begin planning a wind-up the moment the trigger event becomes foreseeable. For complex funds with property or LRBAs, allow a minimum of 18 months. The tax efficiency of your exit depends almost entirely on the time available to sequence it properly.

A Final Note on the SMSF Life Cycle

I want to offer, as we conclude the 9 case-study chapters of this book, a reflection on the SMSF life cycle as I have observed it.

The establishment phase — the excitement of control, the clarity of purpose, the optimism of compounding — is when most trustees are at their most attentive. The ongoing management phase — annual returns, investment reviews, contribution planning, audit compliance — is when the discipline that separates excellent trustees from adequate ones becomes visible. And the wind-up phase — quiet, operational, often unglamorous — is when the full value of everything that came before is either preserved or partially lost.

The trustees I admire most are not those with the cleverest investment strategies or the most sophisticated tax structures (though these matter). They are the ones who understood, from the beginning, that an SMSF is not a product — it is a legal obligation. And who took that obligation seriously enough to keep taking it seriously, year after year, decade after decade, until the job was done.

You are, by virtue of reading this far, clearly one of those people.

The Emotional Dimension of the Wind-Up Decision

Of all the financial decisions associated with an SMSF, the decision to wind it up is uniquely freighted with emotional complexity. For many trustees, the SMSF is not merely a financial structure — it is the tangible expression of years of financial discipline, careful decision-making, and long-term planning. Winding it up can feel like abandoning a project that you invested yourself in, or admitting that the self-managed structure did not ultimately deliver on its promise.

I want to name this dynamic explicitly, because I have seen it cause significant harm. Trustees who delay a necessary wind-up because of the emotional difficulty of closing the structure — who continue to maintain a fund that no longer serves their needs, accumulating compliance costs and administrative burden, simply because they are not ready to let it go — are making a financial decision on emotional grounds. The SMSF does not care about sentiment. The ATO certainly does not.

The appropriate frame for the wind-up decision is this: the SMSF was a tool, deployed in service of a retirement income goal. If the tool continues to serve that goal better than the alternatives, maintain it. If a different tool now serves the goal better — whether because the balance has fallen below the cost-efficient threshold, or because the administrative complexity has exceeded the available energy, or because a life change has made the self-managed structure inappropriate — use the different tool. This is not failure. It is good management.

The trustees I have most admired in this transition are those who made the wind-up decision proactively and deliberately — who assessed their situation clearly, concluded that the cost-benefit no longer favoured the SMSF structure, and planned an orderly exit over twelve to 18 months with the same strategic attention they had applied to every other major SMSF decision. They walked out well. They left with their retirement savings intact, their tax position optimised, and a sense of completion rather than defeat.

Aged Care and the SMSF: A Specific Planning Challenge

One of the most emotionally difficult and practically complex SMSF wind-up scenarios involves the transition of a member to full-time aged care. The cognitive decline that often accompanies aging, combined with the legal and operational requirements of SMSF trusteeship, creates a specific planning challenge that many families encounter unprepared.

The SIS Act requires that all trustees of an SMSF have legal capacity to act as trustees. A member who has lost the cognitive capacity to exercise trustee judgment — due to dementia, stroke, or other cognitive impairment — can no longer legally act as a trustee. The fund must either appoint a replacement trustee (typically a family member acting under an enduring power of attorney) or wind up within a prescribed period.

> **Cognitive Decline and SMSF Trusteeship**
>
> A trustee who lacks legal capacity cannot exercise the duties of trusteeship. If a member's cognitive capacity is declining: • An Enduring Power of Attorney (EPOA) granted before capacity is lost can allow a trusted person to act as trustee in the member's place • The EPOA must be granted while the member retains legal capacity • The SMSF trust deed must expressly permit trustee appointment under EPOA • Without a valid EPOA, wind-up may be the only legal option If you are over 65 or have any health concerns, consider granting an EPOA now, while you have full capacity to do so.

The families I have worked with who navigated this situation most successfully were those who had established the enduring power of attorney well before it was needed — typically as part of their general estate planning review, at the same time they were establishing or updating their will and BDBN. The EPOA was in place, the trust deed permitted its use, and when cognitive decline made it impossible for the member to continue exercising trustee judgment personally, the transition was clean and legally straightforward.

The families who had not done this planning faced a legal tangle: the fund's assets were legally vested in a trustee who could no longer act, and the only pathway involved court applications for guardianship, legal challenges to transaction validity, and administrative costs that consumed a significant portion of the fund's assets during the resolution process.

If you are over 60 and have not yet granted an enduring power of attorney, I encourage you to treat this as a matter of priority equal in urgency to reviewing your BDBN. The probability that you will need it is significant. The cost of establishing it is trivial. And the cost of not having it — to you and to the family members who will be left trying to manage a complex legal structure on your behalf without the legal tools to do so — is potentially enormous.

The Partial Wind-Up: Restructuring Rather Than Closing

Not every wind-up decision involves closing the SMSF entirely. In some circumstances, a partial wind-up — the departure of 1 member from a multi-member fund — is the appropriate response to a changed situation.

The most common scenario: a married couple's SMSF, where one spouse predeceases the other, leaving the surviving spouse as the sole member. The fund can continue as a sole-member SMSF. The question of whether it should is one that the surviving spouse should address with their adviser within the first year following the bereavement.

A second common scenario: a multi-member SMSF where 1 member decides to exit — due to a divorce, an overseas relocation, or a change in their investment preferences — while the remaining member(s) wish to continue. The exiting member's benefit must be rolled out to an alternative fund, and the trust deed may need to be amended to reflect the change in membership. The remaining member(s) continue with the fund, which may now have a smaller balance that warrants a reassessment of the cost-benefit.

The partial wind-up requires the same careful attention to asset valuation, benefit calculation, and rollover administration as a full wind-up. The key difference is that the fund's compliance history continues uninterrupted, which can avoid the restart costs and administrative complexity of establishing a new fund.

Lessons from Wind-Ups: The Patterns I Keep Seeing

In 10 years of practice, I have overseen or reviewed the wind-up of many SMSFs. The pattern of avoidable costs and complications that I observe is remarkably consistent. Let me share the ten most frequent wind-up errors, in descending order of financial cost.

Rank	Error	Typical Cost
1	Forced asset sale under time pressure (overseas move, health event, divorce)	$20,000 – $150,000 in unrealised discount
2	ECPI method error in wind-up year (segregated vs unsegregated)	$5,000 – $80,000 in unexpected tax
3	Failure to realise capital losses before wind-up	$3,000 – $50,000 in unrecovered loss offsets
4	LRBA settlement complexity (bank delays, consent requirements)	$10,000 – $40,000 in bank and legal fees plus time cost
5	Incorrect benefit component calculation (tax-free vs taxable)	$15,000 – $60,000 in avoidable death benefit tax
6	Late minimum pension payment in wind-up year (ECPI loss)	$10,000 – $100,000 in lost ECPI for year

7	Failure to claim final year franking credit refund	$3,000 – $20,000 in unclaimed credits
8	Incorrect rollover form (receiving fund details error)	$2,000 – $15,000 in correction and reprocessing costs
9	Premature ABN cancellation before final return lodged	$1,000 – $10,000 in reinstatement and correction
10	Trustee disagreement during wind-up (divorce or estate dispute)	$20,000 – $200,000+ in legal costs

Eight of the ten most costly errors are preventable with adequate planning time and competent professional support. Numbers one and ten — forced sales under time pressure and trustee disagreements — have an irreducible human dimension that planning can mitigate but not eliminate. The other eight are purely technical: they arise from inadequate preparation, insufficient professional guidance, or insufficient time to execute the wind-up optimally.

The consistent message of every wind-up case I have reviewed is identical to the message of every compliance failure case described in this book: start planning earlier than you think you need to. The last-minute wind-up, like the last-minute compliance fix, is almost always more expensive than the version that began with adequate lead time.

Epilogue

Nine Chapters, Nine Truths, One Decision

We began this book at a dinner party. Marcus, the self-made property developer, who had built an SMSF through discipline and professional advice and arrived at retirement with more than he had imagined possible. Linda, the accountant, who had managed her fund with the quiet consistency of someone who understood what compounding actually meant over 25 years. Richard, the former physician, who had made a series of decisions that seemed reasonable in the moment and catastrophic in aggregate — and who arrived at the conversation with a figure in his mind that he could not quite bring himself to say out loud.

I told you then that this book would not teach you to be Marcus or Linda. I was wrong, slightly. It will not make the decisions for you. But it will, if you have read it carefully and honestly, give you the specific knowledge to avoid being Richard.

Let me distil the nine chapters into the truths that I believe matter most — not because they summarise the technical content (the tables and case studies exist for that), but because they are the principles that I have seen, over 10 years, make the most difference between the trustees who finish well and the ones who don't.

Truth One: The Structure Is Not the Strategy

An SMSF is a vehicle. Like any vehicle, its value depends entirely on where you drive it, how you maintain it, and whether you have a destination in mind. I have watched people establish an SMSF with elaborate trust deed provisions and sophisticated corporate trustee structures — and then leave $800,000 sitting in a high-interest savings account for 4 years because they couldn't agree on what to invest in. The structure was perfect. The outcome was mediocre.

The trustees who do best are those who recognise that establishing the fund is perhaps the easiest step — and that every subsequent decision, from investment strategy to contribution planning to death benefit nominations, is where the real work happens.

Truth Two: Ignorance Is Not a Defence — But It Is Remediable

The ATO does not give a discount for good intentions. The trustee who genuinely did not know about the sole purpose test, or the related party acquisition rules, or the in-house asset limit, is assessed the same penalty as the trustee who knew and ignored the rules. This is not cruel. It is the nature of a legal obligation. Trustees agree, when they sign the trustee declaration, that they have read and understood the rules. The law holds them to that agreement.

But here is the equally important counterpoint: ignorance is completely remediable. Every breach this book describes — every fine, every tax liability, every family conflict — could have been prevented by knowledge. Not by expensive knowledge. Not by years of legal training. By the kind of disciplined, professional, ongoing engagement with qualified advisers that any reasonable person can choose to maintain.

The question is not 'Do I have the time to understand all of this?' The question is 'Do I have the time to pay for not understanding it?' The trustees in this book who suffered the largest losses paid, in my estimation, between 5 and 50 times what the relevant professional advice would have cost.

Truth Three: The Sole Purpose Test Is Not a Technicality — It Is the Point

Section 62 of the SIS Act is sometimes described as if it were a minor compliance checkbox. It is not. It is the entire moral and legal foundation of superannuation. The tax advantages of the superannuation system — the concessional rates, the ECPI exemption, the tax-free pension — exist because the government has decided to incentivise long-term retirement saving. The sole purpose test is the mechanism by which those advantages are restricted to funds that are actually used for that purpose.

When trustees use their SMSF as a tax shelter for business assets, a mechanism for acquiring holiday property, or a vehicle for providing financial benefits to family members, they are not exploiting a loophole. They are transferring to themselves benefits that the tax system created for a different purpose. The ATO pursues these cases vigorously because the integrity of the broader system depends on enforcement.

Understanding this principle — not just as a rule to comply with but as a genuine rationale — changes how trustees approach borderline decisions. The question is not 'Will I get caught?' The question is 'Is this genuinely for my retirement?'

Truth Four: The Tax Advantages Are Real, Substantial, and Fragile

The mathematics of superannuation are extraordinary. A dollar invested in accumulation phase, earning 7% annually, paying 15% tax on earnings, over 30 years, produces more than 3 times the outcome of the same dollar in a personal investment account paying 45% tax on earnings. The pension phase is even more powerful — zero tax on earnings, zero tax on capital gains, zero tax on pension payments after age 60. These are not marginal advantages. They are transformative.

But they are also fragile. Every chapter in this book contains at least one example of how these advantages can be accidentally surrendered — through a NALI determination, a failed sole purpose test, a mismanaged contribution, an excess transfer balance amount. The tax architecture of superannuation rewards precision. It punishes imprecision with penalties that are specifically designed to deter the behaviour they target.

Treat the tax advantages of your SMSF with the same respect you would give to any valuable asset. They require maintenance. They require periodic review. They require professional support. And they repay that investment — in some cases, literally millions of dollars of return over a trustee's lifetime.

Truth Five: Your Investment Strategy Is a Legal Document, Not a Wish List

I have reviewed hundreds of SMSF investment strategies. The worst of them are aspirational paragraphs that describe the trustees' preferences in vague language and bear no demonstrable relationship to what the fund actually holds. The best of them are living documents — specific, quantitative, reviewed and updated annually, and clearly connected to the fund's actual investment decisions.

The ATO requires an investment strategy that considers risk, return, liquidity, diversification, and insurance. It does not require a work of literature. It requires evidence that the trustees have genuinely thought about how the fund's assets are deployed and whether that deployment is appropriate for the members' needs.

When you update your portfolio, update your strategy. When your members' ages and retirement timelines change, update your strategy. When market conditions require you to shift allocation, update your strategy. The discipline of maintaining this document is not bureaucratic box-ticking. It is the ongoing discipline of thinking about whether your current portfolio still makes sense.

Truth Six: Insurance Is Not Optional — It Is Part of the Plan

James's story — the surgeon who became permanently disabled from a cycling accident without TPD insurance inside his SMSF — is the one that haunts me most in this book. Not because it was dramatic. Because it was so ordinary. He was a healthy, accomplished professional who assumed his health would continue. He made no decision about insurance. He simply did not think about it. And that non-decision cost him, and his family, everything.

Insurance inside superannuation is not a product that benefits financial advisers at the expense of their clients. It is the mechanism by which a sudden, catastrophic change in circumstances — a diagnosis, an accident, a death — does not also destroy the financial foundation that everything else depends on. For many members, the combination of life insurance and TPD coverage inside superannuation, funded by pre-tax contributions, is the most cost-effective protection they will ever purchase.

Review your insurance every 3 years. Review it every time your income, debt, dependants, or health status changes significantly. And if you have made a conscious decision not to hold insurance inside your SMSF — because you hold it elsewhere, because your assets are sufficient to self-insure, because your circumstances make it genuinely redundant — document that decision in your investment strategy. A documented decision is not a problem. An undocumented non-decision is a liability waiting to mature.

Truth Seven: Death Benefits Planning Is Not Morbid — It Is Loving

I have tried, in every client meeting where we discuss death benefit nominations, to reframe the conversation. It is not a conversation about death. It is a conversation about love. About making sure that the people you care about most — your spouse, your children, your partner — are protected and provided for in the worst moment of their lives. That the financial catastrophe does not compound the personal catastrophe. That the money goes where you intended, in the amount you intended, with the minimum possible tax consequence.

A binding death benefit nomination, properly executed and regularly renewed, is one of the most loving things you can do as an SMSF trustee. It takes 30 minutes. It costs a few hundred dollars in legal fees. It makes a potentially enormous difference — the difference between Arthur's children receiving nothing and them receiving what their father always intended.

Do it this year. Review it in 3 years. And make sure your will is aligned with it.

Truth Eight: The Exit Is as Important as the Entry

We spend so much energy on the establishment of SMSFs — the structure, the deed, the strategy, the setup. We spend so little energy on the exit. But the exit is where the value of everything that came before is either fully realised or partially lost.

William's wind-up under time pressure cost $47,000 in avoidable costs because the trigger event arrived before the planning did. Patricia's minor administrative oversight created 4 months of delay and unexpected tax. Both outcomes were preventable. Both required only that the trustees start planning before the event forced their hand.

Think now about your exit scenario. Is it an overseas move, in three to 5 years? Is it a retirement transition, when the complexity may no longer seem worth the cost savings? Is it a health-related event that you hope will never come but that prudent planning should account for? Whatever your plausible scenarios, spend one afternoon with your adviser thinking through the wind-up implications. It will not take long. And it will be worth far more than its cost.

Truth Nine: The Best SMSF Is the One You Can Actually Manage

The final truth is perhaps the most quietly important. I have met trustees who built genuinely sophisticated SMSFs — direct property portfolios, LRBAs, complex tax structures, carefully managed contribution strategies — and managed them with diligence and skill for 10 or 15 years. And I have met trustees who built the same sophisticated SMSFs and then discovered, 3 years in, that the cognitive and administrative load was simply more than they wanted to carry.

An SMSF does not make you a better investor by virtue of existing. It makes you the investment manager. That role suits some people perfectly. It does not suit everyone. And one of the most sophisticated financial decisions you can make is recognising honestly, with clear eyes and no ego involvement, whether the self-managed structure is actually serving you — or whether you are serving it.

If your SMSF is enabling investment strategies that would otherwise be unavailable to you, if it is saving you fee costs that matter to your retirement outcome, if it is giving you estate planning flexibility that is genuinely valuable — then it is working. If it is primarily a source of anxiety, administrative burden, and compliance worry, and if your investment strategy is not materially different from what a retail or industry fund would provide — then perhaps the best decision you can make is a planned, tax-efficient wind-up into a structure that serves your actual needs.

There is no shame in that choice. There is only wisdom.

Three Choices

You have finished this book. You stand now at one of three doors.

The first door: you read, you nodded, you found the case studies instructive — and you will do roughly what you were doing before, with perhaps slightly more awareness of the rules you have been bending. I have seen this choice. It is not my preference for you, but it is your choice to make.

The second door: you read and you realised — specifically, concretely — that there are things you have not done that you should have done. A BDBN that has lapsed. An investment strategy that has not been reviewed in 4 years. Insurance coverage that has not been assessed since your income doubled. A co-trustee arrangement that feels increasingly fragile. This recognition is not a crisis. It is an invitation. Make the appointments. Have the conversations. Fix the specific things that need fixing. This year.

The third door: you read and you realised that you do not yet have an SMSF but that you should seriously consider one. You have the balance, the specific investment intentions, the professional advice relationship, and the willingness to take the trustee obligation seriously. If this is you, the final appendix of this book contains the setup checklist that will structure your initial conversations with a qualified adviser.

Whichever door you walk through, I hope what you take from these pages is not fear — of penalties, of the ATO, of the complexity that pervades every chapter. I hope what you take is competence. The calm, grounded competence of someone who understands what they have built, what it requires, and what it will give them in return.

Ten years in this profession have taught me that most people, given clear information and genuine support, make good decisions about their financial future. You clearly care enough to have read two hundred pages on the subject. That care, translated into specific annual actions, is everything that separates the Marcuses and Lindas from the Richards.

Go be a Marcus. Go be a Linda.

You have more than enough to work with.

— Paul Yang

A Note on the Psychology of Financial Decision-Making

Why the Best Investment Strategy in the World Means Nothing Without the Right Relationship with Risk

I have been hesitant, throughout this book, to lean too heavily on psychological theory. This is a book about SMSF management, not about behavioural finance, and the risk of over-psychologising financial decisions is real — it can become a way of explaining away poor outcomes rather than preventing them. But I would be failing the reader if I did not address, directly and with the weight it deserves, the single most consistent predictor of trustee success that I have observed across 10 years of practice.

It is not intelligence. It is not financial literacy. It is not the quality of professional advice (though this matters enormously). It is emotional regulation — the capacity to make financial decisions based on rational analysis rather than emotional reactivity, particularly in periods of market stress, personal difficulty, or acute time pressure.

The case studies in this book are, in the end, case studies in emotional regulation failure. Michael did not lose his retirement savings because he was ignorant of SMSF law. He lost it because the emotional experience of a recent investment success made him feel invincible, and because the emotional pain of admitting a loss made him hold positions far longer than rational analysis would have justified. Arthur's children did not lose their inheritance because Arthur was careless. He lost it because the emotional discomfort of thinking about death led him to defer the planning conversation indefinitely. Patricia did not encounter a four-month wind-up delay because she was incompetent. She encountered it because the administrative complexity of winding up felt overwhelming, and she managed her anxiety by trusting her accountant completely without providing the thorough pre-wind-up brief that would have prevented the ECPI oversight.

In each case, the emotional experience preceded the financial consequence. Understanding the emotional patterns that produce poor financial decisions is not a luxury for those inclined toward self-reflection. It is a practical necessity for anyone managing significant assets across a decades-long investment horizon.

The Six Emotional Patterns That Damage SMSF Performance

Pattern One: The Competence Halo

The competence halo is the extension of demonstrated success in one domain into an unwarranted confidence in an adjacent domain. The surgeon who is brilliant at diagnosis and has good intuition about people becomes confident that this same intuition will serve them in financial markets. The engineer who builds complex systems efficiently becomes confident that they can manage a complex regulatory structure efficiently. The accountant who understands tax law becomes confident that they understand the specific, highly specialised subset of tax law that governs SMSF management.

All of these people are intelligent. All of them have genuine expertise in their actual domains. The error is the extension of that expertise beyond its boundaries — the assumption that being very good at 100 thing makes you good at all hard things. It does not. The SMSF management environment is sufficiently specialised that genuine expertise requires not just intelligence but specific, practice-based, regularly updated knowledge. The competence halo is the mechanism by which very smart people decline to seek the expertise they actually need.

Pattern Two: Loss Aversion and the Ratchet Effect

Daniel Kahneman and Amos Tversky's foundational work on loss aversion established that the psychological pain of a loss is approximately twice as intense as the equivalent pleasure of a gain. The practical consequence in SMSF management: trustees who are experiencing an unrealised loss on an investment consistently underreact — they hold positions past rational exit points, double down on declining assets, and avoid the mental and emotional pain of realising the loss by pretending the paper loss does not exist.

The ratchet effect describes a related phenomenon: trustees who have experienced a period of strong returns anchor their expectations to that performance level, treating any subsequent underperformance as an acute loss rather than a regression to the mean. They then take disproportionate risk to 'recover' the perceived loss — moving into more speculative investments, increasing concentration, or making decisions that the investment strategy does not support. This is the mechanism behind the crypto investments, the unlisted company exposures, and the concentrated single-property positions that appear repeatedly in the case studies throughout this book.

Pattern Three: The Optimism Bias in Long-Horizon Planning

Human beings are systematically overoptimistic about long-horizon outcomes — particularly outcomes that we have personal agency in creating. This is, in most life contexts, a functional psychological adaptation. It enables goal-setting, perseverance, and the sustained effort required to build anything worthwhile. In financial planning, it produces a specific problem: the systematic underestimation of tail risks.

Every trustee who does not have life insurance inside their SMSF has, at some level, made the calculation that they are unlikely to die prematurely. Every trustee who holds a single property representing 90% of the fund has, at some level, decided that the tenant will continue to pay rent and the property will continue to appreciate. These are optimistic assumptions. They are not unreasonable. But the sequence of outcomes in which they are wrong produces catastrophic results — and the financial planning discipline of specifically testing the downside scenarios, rather than defaulting to the optimistic base case, is both counterintuitive and essential.

I routinely ask clients: 'If the thing you are most hoping will not happen actually happens — the illness, the tenant vacancy, the market decline, the death of your co-trustee — what does your financial situation look like?' The answers are sometimes remarkably uncomfortable, revealing gaps in the plan that the optimistic base case had concealed. The discomfort of the question is precisely its value.

Pattern Four: The Status Quo Bias

The status quo bias is the tendency to prefer the current state of affairs over any change, even when the change would produce a materially better outcome. In SMSF management, it manifests as the reluctance to review an investment strategy that is no longer appropriate, to update a BDBN that has lapsed, to wind up a fund that is no longer cost-effective, or to acknowledge that a professional adviser relationship is no longer serving the fund well.

The status quo bias is maintained by the cognitive cost of change — the mental effort, emotional discomfort, and time required to make a different decision — which feels more immediate and concrete than the diffuse, future benefit of the change. The BDBN that has lapsed does not produce any visible harm today. The review conversation with the adviser costs time and attention that are immediately apparent. The status quo wins by default.

The antidote is systems — specifically, the annual review calendar described in Appendix B of this book. When the review is scheduled and the obligation to address specific items is built into the calendar, the status quo bias must compete with a pre-committed action that has already been planned. Systems consistently outperform willpower in managing behaviour over long time horizons.

Pattern Five: Social Proof and the Investment Fashion Cycle

Human beings are social animals whose judgments of appropriateness are powerfully influenced by what we observe others doing. In financial markets, this manifests as the investment fashion cycle: a class of assets that is attracting positive attention, generating visible returns for early investors, and being discussed positively in social environments produces a growing pressure toward participation that is entirely decoupled from the asset's fundamental value or SMSF investment strategy appropriateness.

The cryptocurrency chapter of the Australian investment story (approximately 2017-2021) was, for SMSF trustees, a textbook demonstration of social proof dynamics. The early adopters produced extraordinary returns that were highly visible in the social environment. The question 'Have you bought any crypto?' became a regular feature of dinner party conversation among a certain demographic of SMSF trustees. The social cost of not participating — the mild social embarrassment of not having 'gotten in' — provided a consistent low-level pressure toward participation. The SMSF investment strategy, which in most cases did not contemplate cryptocurrency investment, became an obstacle to be rationalised rather than a discipline to be observed.

The outcome is well documented: many SMSF trustees who entered the cryptocurrency market at or near peak valuations experienced losses of 50% to 90%. The social proof that had driven their entry evaporated rapidly. The investment strategy they had bypassed turned out to have been well-calibrated.

Pattern Six: The Planning Fallacy and Underestimating Complexity

The planning fallacy — the systematic underestimation of the time, cost, and complexity required to complete a project — applies with particular force in SMSF management. Trustees who decide to establish an SMSF consistently underestimate the time required to maintain it. Those who decide to implement an LRBA consistently underestimate the complexity of the banking, legal, and compliance requirements. Those who decide to wind up consistently underestimate the lead time required for an orderly exit.

The planning fallacy is reinforced by the framing of initial investment decisions. When the decision is made to establish the fund or acquire the property, the focus is on the anticipated upside — the returns, the tax savings, the investment control. The administrative complexity is a background consideration, frequently minimised by advisers eager to facilitate the engagement and by the trustees' own optimism about their ability to manage the ongoing obligations alongside their other professional and personal commitments.

The antidote to the planning fallacy in SMSF management is the same as in project management: reference class forecasting. Before estimating the time and complexity of any significant SMSF decision, ask your adviser how long similar decisions have taken for comparable clients in the past. This data is more reliable than your internal estimate, which is inevitably biased toward the optimistic. Your adviser's experience with fifty similar transactions is a more accurate predictor of your outcome than your hope that yours will be simpler.

The Relationship Between Adviser Trust and Trustee Engagement

One of the most consistent findings in my practice is that the quality of the trustee-adviser relationship is a more powerful predictor of SMSF outcomes than any single technical factor. This does not mean that technical competence is unimportant — it is essential. It means that technical competence, in the absence of a genuine relationship of trust and communication, does not reliably translate into good outcomes for the trustee.

The specific relationship dynamic that produces the best outcomes has several consistent features: the trustee feels comfortable raising concerns and asking questions without feeling judged; the adviser proactively identifies issues and communicates them clearly before they become crises; the annual review is genuinely productive rather than a compliance formality; the adviser and trustee have a shared understanding of the trustee's goals, risk tolerance, and life stage; and the adviser is willing to deliver uncomfortable advice — to say 'this property is too concentrated a position for your fund' or 'your insurance coverage is seriously inadequate' — even when the trustee has emotional resistance to hearing it.

The relationships that produce the worst outcomes have an equally consistent set of features: the trustee does not fully understand what the adviser does on their behalf; the adviser does not proactively communicate potential issues; annual reviews feel like rubber-stamping exercises; the trustee feels that asking questions would reveal ignorance they are embarrassed about; and the adviser's commercial interest in maintaining a fee-generating relationship creates subtle pressure to avoid difficult conversations.

If the second description feels more familiar than the first, I encourage you to reflect on whether your current advisory relationship is actually serving your interests — or whether the comfort of a familiar, low-friction relationship is preventing the conversations that would improve your fund's governance and performance. The most valuable thing I can sometimes tell a client is not a technical insight about their superannuation. It is the observation that their current advisory relationship is not generating the engagement their fund requires.

The Long Game: Thinking in Decades, Not Years

The temporal frame through which you view your SMSF matters enormously. Trustees who evaluate their fund's performance over quarterly or annual periods are playing a different game than those who evaluate it over decades. The short-term frame produces a specific set of behaviours: reactivity to market movements, excessive rebalancing, loss aversion-driven position management, and a constant comparison to short-term benchmarks. The long-term frame produces different behaviours: patience with volatility, willingness to hold positions through market cycles, focus on structural tax efficiency over trading gains, and a consistent attention to the compliance and governance obligations that determine the fund's long-term viability.

The compound arithmetic of superannuation is the most powerful argument for the long-term frame. At 7% annual return, $500,000 becomes $1,000,000 in approximately 10 years. In 10 years, it becomes $1,935,000. In 30 years, $3,745,000. These figures are before the tax advantages of the superannuation environment, which accelerate the compounding further. The trustee who interferes with this compounding — through excessive trading, poor tax management, or compliance failures that generate tax penalties — is working against the most powerful force available to them.

I have seen trustees make decisions worth millions of dollars in 2-minute meetings, without adequate analysis, under the pressure of a market movement or a tax deadline. I have seen other trustees spend days researching a decision worth tens of thousands of dollars, bringing an analytical rigour that was entirely disproportionate to the stakes. The right allocation of attention is the opposite: significant time and professional support for the high-stakes structural decisions (LRBA acquisition, pension commencement, death benefit planning, wind-up), and a system of regular, brief, routine attention for the ongoing compliance obligations that prevent small problems from becoming large ones.

10 Years of Practice: What I Have Learned About What Actually Works

I want to close this section with the simplest possible summary of everything I have learned about what makes the difference between SMSF trustees who finish well and those who do not.

It is not the investment strategy, though investment strategy matters. It is not the tax structure, though the tax structure can add hundreds of thousands of dollars to a retirement outcome. It is not the trust deed, though a good deed provides important legal protections.

What makes the difference — the single variable that most reliably separates good outcomes from poor ones — is engagement. Specifically: genuine, informed, ongoing engagement with both the compliance obligations and the strategic decisions of the fund, supported by competent professional advice, maintained consistently across the full lifecycle of the structure from establishment to wind-up.

Engagement is not the same as obsession. The trustees who do best are not those who are constantly monitoring their portfolio, trading frequently, or spending hours each week on superannuation administration. They are the ones who have built systems that ensure the important things get attention at the right times — and who show up to their annual review prepared, informed, and willing to hear whatever needs to be heard.

Engagement is not the same as DIY. Many of the most engaged trustees I know delegate almost everything to professional advisers. Their engagement manifests as a willingness to be briefed, a habit of asking good questions, and a practice of reviewing the important documents — investment strategy, BDBN, auditor's report — at least annually. They are engaged consumers of expert advice, not would-be experts themselves.

And engagement is not permanent. Life changes. The level of engagement that was easy at 52 may not be sustainable at 72. The appropriate response is not to ignore this reality but to plan for it: to have the conversation with your adviser about succession, about what happens when managing the fund becomes too complex, about at what point the wind-up conversation makes sense. The trustees who have this conversation proactively, on their own terms and timeline, make better decisions than those who have it reactively, when circumstances have already forced the issue.

You are the trustee of your own retirement. The law imposes the obligation, but the choice is yours: to take that obligation seriously, to build the professional relationships and annual systems that give it the attention it requires, and to make the structural decisions — insurance, nominations, investment strategy, exit planning — that protect not just your retirement but the financial wellbeing of the people who depend on you.

The clients I think of most fondly are not the ones with the largest balances. They are the ones who took their trusteeship seriously enough to ask hard questions, who maintained professional relationships that served them well across decades, who planned carefully for the moments of transition, and who arrived at retirement

— or at wind-up — with their fund in good order and their family provided for.

That is what a well-managed SMSF looks like. And it is entirely within your reach.

Case Study Revisited: Sarah's Complete Journey

Throughout this book, Sarah has appeared in brief vignettes — the Chatswood commercial property LRBA, the Vanguard ETF portfolio, the professional management that protected her from the compliance failures that beset Michael. I want, in this final section, to tell Sarah's complete story — from the establishment of her SMSF to her retirement transition at age 62 — as an integrated illustration of everything this book has covered.

The Establishment: Getting the Foundation Right

Sarah was 38 when she and her accountant first discussed the SMSF option. Her superannuation balance was $280,000 — not yet at the conventional threshold, but Sarah had a specific plan: she wanted to acquire a commercial tenancy in a small business precinct in Sydney's upper North, where a physiotherapist had expressed interest in a long-term lease. The business real property rules permitted her SMSF to acquire commercial property from an unrelated vendor, and the related-party tenancy arrangement (subject to arm's length rent) was explicitly permitted.

Sarah's first decision was the corporate trustee. Her accountant recommended it; Sarah agreed without requiring persuasion. The additional setup cost of $1,200 was trivial relative to the fund's scale. The corporate trustee was established as a purpose-specific company with Sarah as sole director.

The trust deed was drafted by an SMSF specialist legal firm, not by a generic document provider. Sarah paid $1,800 for the deed — more than the discount online providers would have charged. The deed included express provisions for non-lapsing BDBNs, pension commencement powers, corporate trustee succession, and the treatment of investment reserves. Sarah did not understand all of these provisions in detail at the time. She trusted the specialist recommendation. She would come to be grateful for several of these provisions over the following 24 years.

The LRBA: Doing It by the Book

The Chatswood commercial property was purchased for $860,000 in Sarah's first year of SMSF operation. She contributed $200,000 in non-concessional contributions to fund the deposit. The LRBA was arranged through a commercial lender at the prevailing commercial property rate. The bare trust was established correctly, with a separate corporate trustee, a separate bank account, and documentation that met all ATO requirements.

The rent from the physiotherapy practice was set at $62,000 per year — the market rate confirmed by 2 independent real estate appraisals. It was reviewed and adjusted annually. When market rents in the precinct increased, Sarah's rent was increased accordingly. Not because she was indifferent to her tenant's financial position — she was not — but because the NALI rules required market-rate rent, and Sarah's adviser had made this requirement unambiguous from the beginning.

The LRBA interest cost fluctuated over the years as rates changed. In the high-rate period of 2022-2025, the fund's annual interest bill reached $71,000 — leaving a modest cash deficit against the $62,000 rental income. Sarah funded the deficit from her Vanguard ETF dividends, which totalled approximately $25,000 per year. The fund never missed a payment, never drew on a capital buffer, and never faced a compliance issue related to the LRBA.

The Contributions: Systematic and Optimised

Sarah maintained maximum concessional contributions throughout her working years, using salary sacrifice to redirect the gap between her employer's SG contribution and the annual cap into the SMSF. In years when she received bonus income, she made non-concessional contributions using the bring-forward rule where available. She tracked her total superannuation balance annually, confirmed her contribution eligibility with her accountant every April, and initiated the final year's contributions by June 15 each year — not June 28.

At age 55 (then the preservation age, broadly comparable to age 60 today), Sarah commissioned a contribution optimisation review. Her adviser identified that her tax-free component was only 31% of her total balance — relatively low, reflecting years of predominantly concessional contributions. They implemented a three-year recontribution strategy: drawing down annually from the fund, paying the applicable tax, and recontributing the after-tax proceeds as non-concessional contributions. By age 58, her tax-free proportion had risen to approximately 54%. The estimated saving in eventual death benefit tax for her adult daughter Emily and adult son Thomas: approximately $48,000.

The Insurance: Protection That Earned Its Premium

Sarah held $1.2 million in life insurance and $800,000 in TPD (any occupation) inside the SMSF from the fund's establishment, funded through salary sacrifice contributions. She reviewed the coverage every 3 years. At age 50, when her mortgage was paid off, she reduced the life insurance to $900,000 — eliminating the premium cost associated with mortgage debt replacement, which was no longer needed. Her TPD coverage remained at $800,000 throughout.

At age 53, Sarah was diagnosed with an autoimmune condition that, while manageable, would have been uninsurable as a new condition had she not already held the TPD policy. The diagnosis did not affect her ability to continue working — the condition was well-controlled — but it gave her a vivid appreciation of the insurance coverage she had, and the financial catastrophe that would have followed had she been uninsured and the condition progressed to disability. She never missed an insurance premium renewal after that.

The Death Benefits: Planning for the Inevitable

Sarah's husband David was not an SMSF member — his superannuation was managed through his employer's industry fund. Sarah's death benefit planning was therefore centred on 2 scenarios: death before retirement (most benefit going to David), and death after retirement (with adult children Emily and Thomas as non-dependent beneficiaries).

Sarah executed a non-lapsing BDBN at fund establishment and reviewed it at every annual meeting. The nomination directed 100% of the death benefit to her legal personal representative in the event of her death after retirement — with the estate plan (a carefully drafted will with testamentary trust provisions) directing the benefit to Emily and Thomas through the testamentary trust. The testamentary trust provided significant income-splitting advantages for the grandchildren's education expenses in the years following Sarah's eventual death.

The Transition: Pension Commencement at Age 60

At age 60, Sarah commenced an account-based pension from the full balance that was within her Transfer Balance Cap. Her financial adviser had modelled the TBC position carefully: at pension commencement, her balance was $1.86 million — within the $1.9 million TBC with comfortable margin. The remaining accumulation balance of approximately $320,000 continued in accumulation phase, with the pension balance generating tax-free income under the ECPI segregated method.

The Chatswood commercial property — now owned outright by the SMSF (the LRBA had been fully repaid at age 57) — was included in the pension segment at its current market value of $2.1 million, resetting the cost base. Any future sale of the property would generate a fully CGT-exempt capital gain.

The Outcome: 24 Years Later

When Sarah turned 62, her SMSF had a total value of approximately $3.85 million. Her annual pension income of $185,000 — drawn at the minimum rate, tax-free after age 60 — comfortably exceeded her retirement income target. The Chatswood property's rental income alone, at $115,000 per year, covered most of the pension payment. The ETF portfolio provided additional income and liquidity.

She had paid a total of approximately $216,000 in professional SMSF management costs over 24 years ($3,700 per year on average, rising over time). Against a starting balance of $280,000 and ending balance of $3.85 million — a growth of $3.57 million — the professional management cost represented 6% of the total gain. The return on the investment in expert advice was, by any reasonable measure, extraordinary.

Sarah's SMSF was not a spectacular story of exceptional market timing or genius investment selection. It was a story of structural soundness, compliance discipline, tax optimisation, and the consistent application of expertise across 2 decades. It was the story that is available to every SMSF trustee who approaches the structure with the seriousness it deserves.

> **$3,570,000 Sarah's Net Wealth Creation Over 24 Years**
>
> From $280,000 initial balance to $3.85M — net gain of $3.57M over 24 years. Professional management cost: $216,000 (6% of total gain). Return on advice investment: 16.5x.

From Here: Your Next Three Actions

This book has covered a great deal of ground. If you have read it in full — or even selectively, focusing on the chapters most relevant to your current situation — you have a substantially better understanding of the SMSF framework than the majority of trustees currently managing their own funds. That knowledge is worth something. But it is only worth something if it translates into action.

I want to close with a very specific request: identify three concrete actions from this book that you will take in the next 90 days. Not aspirational resolutions — specific, calendar-dated actions with a nominated responsible party (you, your adviser, your solicitor) and a target completion date.

The most commonly identified actions by trustees who have worked through this material are: scheduling an annual review meeting with their SMSF adviser to cover the topics in Chapter Seven's contributions checklist and Chapter Eight's death benefit checklist; reviewing and updating the BDBN if it has lapsed or if the named beneficiaries' circumstances have changed; and commissioning an independent insurance needs analysis if the fund's current coverage has not been formally reviewed in the past 3 years.

These three actions, completed within 90 days, will address three of the most common and most costly compliance gaps in the Australian SMSF landscape. They are not complex. They do not require exceptional financial sophistication. They require only the decision to act — and the calendar discipline to follow through.

The difference between a well-governed SMSF and a poorly governed one is, in the end, the accumulation of small, specific, time-stamped actions: reviewing the strategy, renewing the nomination, testing the insurance, attending the annual meeting prepared. Each action is individually modest. Together, across a ten-year investment horizon, they are worth millions of dollars.

You know what to do. Now do it.

Appendix A
SMSF Establishment Checklist

Everything You Need Before and After Setting Up Your Fund

This checklist is designed for use in your first meeting with a qualified SMSF adviser. Not every item will be relevant immediately — some are day-one tasks, others are month-three or month-twelve tasks. But having the complete list in front of you from the beginning ensures that nothing critical is deferred indefinitely.

Phase 1: Pre-Establishment (Before You Sign Anything)

Task	Notes	Done
Confirm minimum balance ($200K+ recommended)	Below this threshold, cost efficiency is usually poor vs retail/industry fund	☐
Identify all proposed members (max 6)	All members must be eligible; check any disqualified person issues	☐
Decide on trustee structure: individual vs corporate trustee	Corporate trustee strongly recommended for funds with 2+ members or significant assets	☐
Engage an SMSF-specialist financial adviser	Verify they hold an AFSL with SMSF authority; check ASIC register	☐
Engage an SMSF-specialist accountant/tax agent	The same firm as your financial adviser, or	☐

	coordinated between separate firms	
Confirm specific investment intentions that require SMSF	Property LRBA, direct shares, business real property — what specifically can't you do in retail/industry fund?	☐
Clarify estate planning goals	Who are your intended death benefit beneficiaries? Are they dependants?	☐
Review current superannuation balances and components	Tax-free vs taxable component ratio; potential for recontribution strategy	☐
Obtain insurance needs analysis	What life/TPD/income protection coverage do you need? What is appropriate inside vs outside SMSF?	☐

Phase 2: Establishment (Day 1–Day 30)

Task	Notes	Done
Execute trust deed (via solicitor or specialist deed provider)	Ensure deed permits non-lapsing BDBNs if desired; confirm pension commencement powers	☐
Register corporate trustee with ASIC (if using)	All directors must be eligible; ASIC annual fee applies ($57 currently)	☐

Apply for ABN and TFN for the fund	Via ATO business registration portal or tax agent	☐
Open dedicated fund bank account	Account must be in name of trustee(s) in their capacity as trustee; separate from personal accounts	☐
Sign trustee declaration (NAT 71089)	All trustees must sign within 21 days of becoming trustee; retain indefinitely	☐
Prepare written investment strategy	Must address risk, return, liquidity, diversification, and insurance	☐
Execute Binding Death Benefit Nominations for all members	Correctly witnessed; calendar renewal reminder (3 years unless non-lapsing)	☐
Register for GST if applicable (e.g., fund owns commercial property)	Threshold applies; confirm with accountant	☐
Roll over existing superannuation balances to the SMSF	Obtain rollover forms; confirm receiving fund details; allow 3–5 business days	☐

Phase 3: Ongoing Compliance (Annual Tasks)

Task	Timing	Done
Review and update investment strategy	July–August each year	☐
Confirm minimum pension payments will be met before June 30	April–May each year	☐
Review contribution levels vs caps (concessional and non-concessional)	April each year (pre-year-end planning)	☐
Confirm work test compliance if members aged 67–74 are claiming a tax deduction for personal contributions	Evidence documented by June 30	☐
Obtain independent valuations of all non-listed assets	By June 30 each year (required for audit)	☐
Review BDBN validity dates	At least 30 days before any 3-year anniversary	☐
Commission annual audit by approved SMSF auditor	Must be completed before annual return lodgement	☐
Lodge SMSF annual return with ATO	By due date (typically October 31, or later with tax agent)	☐

Pay ASIC annual fee (corporate trustee)	Invoice issued annually; pay promptly to avoid deregistration	☐
Review insurance coverage for all members	At least every 3 years or after major life changes	☐
Assess transfer balance cap usage for all pension members	Confirm no excess TBC issues; model for future year	☐

Appendix B

The SMSF Annual Compliance Calendar

Month-by-Month Actions for Trustees Who Plan Ahead

This calendar is designed to eliminate the January panic — the calls I receive every February from trustees who realise they have not yet paid their minimum pension, or that their June 30 contribution has not been planned. The goal is proactive management: addressing each compliance obligation at the optimal time, not the last possible moment.

Month	Key Action	Consequences of Deferring
July	Open new financial year; confirm opening pension balances for minimum payment calculation; update contribution caps	Miscalculated minimum pension; contribution cap errors
August	Review and update investment strategy; confirm all assets have current valuations	Non-compliant investment strategy; audit issues
September	Review insurance coverage; check BDBN expiry dates; confirm ASIC corporate trustee fee is paid	Lapsed insurance or BDBN; ASIC deregistration risk
October	Prior year SMSF annual return due (if lodging without tax agent); review prior year audit findings	Late lodgement penalties

November	Mid-year portfolio review; assess whether rebalancing is needed before year-end	Suboptimal year-end position
December	Review concessional contributions YTD; model remaining cap space; confirm salary sacrifice arrangements	Contribution cap breach if not modelled
January	Confirm minimum pension payments to date; assess whether sufficient cash is available for remainder of year	Minimum pension shortfall risk — serious consequences
February	Review non-concessional contributions; assess bring-forward eligibility if large contribution planned	NCC cap breach; excess contribution tax
March	Obtain independent valuations for direct property and other non-listed assets (allows time to dispute if low)	Audit qualification if no current valuations at June 30
April	Year-end planning meeting with adviser: contributions, CGT events, ECPI management, final pension payments	Missed optimisation opportunities
May	Execute final contributions for the year (must be received in fund	Settlement timing risk if left to last week

	by June 30); confirm lump sum withdrawals if needed	
June	Final pension payment for the year (if not paid monthly); confirm minimum pensions complete; review any outstanding compliance actions	Loss of ECPI for year if minimum pension not paid

Appendix C
Key Legislative References

The Rules Behind the Rules

This appendix summarises the primary legislative references that underpin the rules and principles discussed throughout this book. It is not a substitute for professional legal advice — the legislation is complex, and its application to specific circumstances requires qualified interpretation. But having a basic familiarity with these references will make your conversations with advisers more productive.

Reference	What It Governs	Relevant Chapter
SIS Act s62 — Sole Purpose Test	Requires that an SMSF be maintained for the sole purpose of providing retirement, death, or disability benefits. No collateral benefits to related parties.	Chapter 4
SIS Act s65 — Prohibition on Financial Assistance to Members	Trustees cannot lend fund assets to members or their relatives. No exceptions.	Chapter 4
SIS Act s66 — Prohibition on Acquisition of Assets from Related Parties	Trustees generally cannot acquire assets from related parties. Key exceptions: listed securities, business real property, widely held unit trusts.	Chapter 4

SIS Act s71 — In-House Asset Limit	No more than 5% of fund assets may be invested in 'in-house assets' — assets that are loans to, or investments in, a related party.	Chapter 4
SIS Act s52B — Trustee Covenants (Investment Strategy)	Trustees must formulate, review, and give effect to an investment strategy having regard to risk, return, liquidity, diversification, and insurance.	Chapters 3, 4
SISR Regulation 13.18AA — Collectibles and Personal Use Assets	Strict rules for SMSFs holding art, wine, jewellery, vehicles, and similar assets. Storage, insurance, and use restrictions apply.	Chapter 4
ITAA 1997 s295-465 — Non-Arm's Length Income (NALI)	Income from non-arm's length arrangements assessed at 45%. Post-2019 amendments extend to non-arm's length expenses.	Chapters 3, 5
ITAA 1997 Div 294 — Transfer Balance Tax	Excess transfer balance amounts are taxed. Assessed on notional earnings of the excess during the period it remained in retirement phase.	Chapter 7

ITAA 1997 s301 — Death Benefit Tax	Superannuation lump sum death benefits paid to non-dependants: taxable component taxed at 15% (plus 2% Medicare levy). Dependants receive tax-free.	Chapter 8
SIS Act s104 — Binding Death Benefit Nominations	Formal requirements for BDBNs; must comply with deed and regulations; lapse after 3 years unless deed provides otherwise.	Chapter 8
SIS Act ss17A–17B — Residency Requirements	Fund must have central management and control in Australia; active members must be Australian residents. Two-year safe harbour for temporary overseas absence.	Chapter 9
SIS Act s35B — Annual Audit Requirement	Every SMSF must have its accounts and compliance audited annually by an approved SMSF auditor.	All chapters
Superannuation (Excess Concessional Contributions) Tax Act 2007	Excess concessional contributions are included in assessable income at marginal rate, with a 15% tax offset and interest charge.	Chapter 7

Appendix D
Glossary of Key Terms

Plain-Language Definitions for the Specialist Language of SMSFs

Term	Definition
Accumulation phase	The stage of superannuation in which a member's balance is building through contributions and investment returns. Tax rate on earnings: 15%.
Account-based pension	A regular income stream from superannuation commenced after meeting a condition of release. Minimum annual drawdown percentages apply by age.
Approved SMSF auditor	A person registered with ASIC to audit SMSF financial accounts and compliance. Must be independent of the fund's trustees.
Binding Death Benefit Nomination (BDBN)	A formal written direction to trustees specifying who receives the member's death benefit. Trustees must comply if the nomination is valid.
Business real property	Land and buildings used wholly and exclusively in a business. SMSFs can acquire business real property from related parties — an exception to the related party acquisition rule.

Bring-forward rule	A provision allowing eligible members (under age 75 at July 1, extended from 67 from 1 July 2022) to contribute up to 3 years' non-concessional contributions in a single year.
Capital gains tax (CGT)	Tax on the gain made when a capital asset is sold or disposed of. Inside an SMSF: 15% in accumulation phase (10% after 12 months); 0% in pension phase.
Central management and control	The high-level strategic decision-making of a trust or company. Must ordinarily be exercised in Australia for SMSF residency compliance.
Condition of release	A legal event (such as retirement, reaching age 65, or permanent incapacity) that allows a member to access their superannuation benefits.
Concessional contributions	Before-tax contributions to superannuation (employer SG, salary sacrifice, personal deductible). Taxed at 15% inside the fund. Annual cap: $30,000 (2024-25).
Corporate trustee	A company that acts as trustee of an SMSF instead of individual members. Provides continuity of ownership and better administrative outcomes.

Defined benefit fund	A superannuation fund that pays a predetermined benefit based on salary and years of service. Not an SMSF. Different rules apply.
Diversification	Spreading investments across different asset classes, sectors, and geographies to reduce concentration risk. Required consideration in the investment strategy.
Downsizer contribution	A contribution to superannuation from the sale of a principal residence, available to members aged 55+. Up to $300,000 per person; outside the NCC cap.
ECPI (Exempt Current Pension Income)	Income and capital gains earned on assets supporting pension liabilities that are exempt from income tax. Two methods: segregated and unsegregated.
Franking credit	A tax credit attached to dividends paid by Australian companies that have already paid corporate tax. Can be claimed by the SMSF to offset tax liability.
In-house asset	A loan to, or investment in, a related party of the SMSF. Subject to a 5% cap on fund assets. Exceeding the cap triggers compliance obligations.
Legal personal representative (LPR)	The executor of a deceased person's estate (or the court-

	appointed administrator if there is no will). A valid BDBN beneficiary in superannuation.
Limited recourse borrowing arrangement (LRBA)	A mechanism allowing an SMSF to borrow money to acquire a single asset (or collection of identical assets). The lender's recourse is limited to the acquired asset.
Minimum pension	The minimum annual amount that must be paid from an account-based pension, calculated as a percentage of the opening balance by the member's age.
NALI (Non-Arm's Length Income)	Income from a scheme where the parties are not dealing at arm's length and the SMSF receives a greater benefit than it would from an arm's length dealing. Taxed at 45%.
Non-concessional contributions (NCC)	After-tax contributions to superannuation. No tax applied on entry. Annual cap: $120,000 (2025–26). Subject to Total Superannuation Balance limits.
Non-lapsing BDBN	A binding death benefit nomination that does not expire after 3 years. Available if the trust deed expressly permits it.
Pension phase (Retirement phase)	The stage of superannuation in which a member draws an income stream. Earnings and gains on

	supporting assets are tax-exempt under ECPI.
Preservation age	The age at which a member can access their superannuation (currently 60 for anyone born on or after 1 July 1964).
Proportional rule	A rule requiring that every superannuation payment (withdrawal or death benefit) contains the same ratio of tax-free to taxable components as the account balance.
Related party	A member of the SMSF, a trustee, or an associate of either. Dealings with related parties are heavily restricted to prevent conflicts of interest.
Reversionary pension	An account-based pension that automatically reverts to a nominated beneficiary (usually a spouse) on the member's death, continuing without interruption.
SIS Act	Superannuation Industry (Supervision) Act 1993 — the primary legislation governing SMSF operations, investment rules, and trustee obligations.
Sole purpose test	The requirement that an SMSF is maintained solely to provide retirement, death, or disability benefits to members or their beneficiaries (SIS Act s62).

Superannuation Guarantee (SG)	The minimum employer contribution required by law. 12% for 2025–26 (increased from 11.5% in 2024–25).
Tax-free component	The portion of a member's superannuation balance representing contributions that were not taxed on entry (non-concessional contributions). No tax on withdrawal or as death benefit.
Taxable component	The portion of a member's superannuation balance representing concessional contributions, employer contributions, and fund earnings. Subject to tax when paid to non-dependants.
Testamentary trust	A trust created by a will that comes into existence on the testator's death. Provides tax-efficient distribution of estate assets, including superannuation death benefits flowing through the estate.
Total Superannuation Balance (TSB)	The total of a member's superannuation balances across all funds, plus certain outstanding LRBA amounts. Used to determine eligibility for NCC, bring-forward, and catch-up contributions.
Transfer Balance Cap (TBC)	The lifetime limit on the total amount of superannuation benefits

	that can be transferred into retirement phase. Currently $1.9 million (2023-24 onwards, subject to indexation).
Trust deed	The legal document establishing the SMSF, setting out the rules by which the fund is governed. Must comply with superannuation legislation and be regularly reviewed.
Trustee declaration (NAT 71089)	An ATO form that all new individual trustees and directors of corporate trustees must sign within 21 days, confirming they understand their obligations.
Wind-up	The formal process of ceasing the operation of an SMSF, including realising assets, paying member benefits, completing final compliance obligations, and cancelling the fund's ABN.
Work test	A requirement for members aged 67–74 to have worked at least 40 hours in any 30 consecutive days in the financial year to be eligible to make personal contributions.

Appendix E

Questions to Ask Your SMSF Adviser

A Trustee's Due Diligence Framework

The relationship between an SMSF trustee and their professional adviser is one of the most important financial relationships you will maintain. The adviser holds knowledge that you will likely never fully replicate. But the trustee holds decision-making authority and accountability that cannot be delegated. The best outcomes emerge from a genuine partnership — where the adviser has deep expertise and the trustee has the knowledge to ask the right questions.

Use this list at your first meeting with any new SMSF adviser, and revisit the most relevant questions at your annual review.

Questions About the Adviser's Qualifications and Approach

Question	What You're Looking For
What specific SMSF qualifications and experience do you hold?	Look for: AFSL with SMSF authority, CAANZ or CPA membership, SMSF Specialist Adviser (SSA) designation from SMSF Association
Do you operate your own SMSF?	Personal experience is not mandatory, but it indicates genuine commitment to the structure
How many SMSF clients do you currently service?	Both too few (<10) and too many (>300 per adviser) can be concerns; ask about the support team structure

How do you charge for your services?	Transparency on fee structure (hourly, fixed, percentage of assets) is essential; understand what you pay for
Do you outsource any compliance functions, and if so, to whom?	Understand the full team involved in your fund's management

Questions About Your Fund's Compliance

Question	What You're Looking For
Is our current investment strategy compliant? When was it last updated?	Should be reviewed at least annually; should reference specific assets held
Are all our related party transactions documented at arm's length?	Any transaction with a related party should have contemporaneous evidence of market-rate pricing
Are all our BDBN nominations current and correctly executed?	Check dates; check witnessing; check that beneficiaries are eligible
What is our current ECPI method, and is it appropriate for our fund?	Segregated vs unsegregated; implications for the current year and planned changes
Have any audit findings or ATO queries been raised in the past 3 years?	How were they resolved? What was the preventative action taken?
What is our current non-concessional contribution room for each member?	Based on TSB and current cap; confirm before any large contribution

Are any of our assets subject to NALI risk?	Any arrangement with a related party should be assessed

Questions About Future Planning

Question	What You're Looking For
What is the optimal contribution strategy for the next 3 years?	Concessional, non-concessional, catch-up, downsizer — which applies and in what order?
When should we commence pension phase, and what are the TBC implications?	Model TBC usage; confirm reversionary pension nominations
What is our estimated death benefit tax exposure for non-dependent beneficiaries?	Understand tax-free vs taxable component ratio; explore recontributioh strategy
What is our plan if 1 trustee dies, becomes incapacitated, or moves overseas?	Business continuity; corporate trustee advantage; wind-up timeline if needed
At what balance or life stage would you recommend we consider winding up?	Cost-benefit analysis relative to alternatives; what would trigger a recommendation to wind up?
How does our SMSF integrate with our overall estate plan?	Confirm alignment of BDBN, reversionary pensions, will, and testamentary trust provisions

These questions will not always produce comfortable conversations. Advisers who have not reviewed your investment strategy recently, or who cannot explain your ECPI method confidently, or who are uncertain about your BDBN validity — these are not necessarily cause for alarm. They are an invitation for action. Every gap identified is a gap that can be closed.

The purpose of a good advisory relationship is not to find out that everything is perfect. It is to find out what needs to be improved — and to improve it.

This book is for educational purposes only and does not constitute financial, legal, or taxation advice. The case studies presented are illustrative composites based on common SMSF trustee experiences. Individual circumstances vary, and all financial decisions should be made in consultation with a qualified professional holding the appropriate Australian Financial Services Licence. The legislative references and contribution caps cited reflect the 2025-26 financial year and are subject to change through annual indexation and legislative amendment.

www.ingramcontent.com/pod-product-compliance
Lightning Source LLC
LaVergne TN
LVHW022156200926
848481LV00006B/1762